TOTAL LIBERATION

TOTAL LIBERATION

Zen Spirituality and the Social Dimension

Ruben L. F. Habito

ORBIS BOOKS

Maryknoll, New York 10545

An earlier version of this book was published by the Zen Center for Oriental Spirituality in the Philippines. Copyright © 1986 by the Zen Center for Oriental Spirituality in the Philippines, Provident Village, Marikina, Metro Manila, Philippines.

Revised and expanded edition published 1989 by Orbis Books, Maryknoll, NY 10545.
Copyright © 1989 by Ruben L. F. Habito
All rights reserved
Manufactured in the United States of America

Manuscript editor: Joan Laflamme

Library of Congress Cataloging-in-Publication Data

Habito, Ruben L. F., 1947–
    Total liberation: Zen spirituality and the social dimension/
Ruben L. F. Habito.
    p. cm.
    ISBN 0-88344-537-9
    1. Zen Buddhism—Doctrines. 2. Zen Buddhism—Relations—Catholic Church 3. Catholic Church—Relations—Zen Buddhism. I. Title
BQ9268.7.H3 1989   89-2863
294.3'927—dc19   CIP

To
Maria-Kannon

Contents

Foreword

It is with great joy that I offer a foreword to the compilation of Zen material by Ruben Habito. When Ruben Habito arrived in Japan in 1970, he almost immediately became involved in Zen. He was, as far as I know, the first Catholic to have received confirmation of the opening Zen experience (*Kenshō*) under a Japanese Zen Master. Since then he has assiduously maintained his training under this true teacher, Yamada Kōun Rōshi of the Kamakura San-un Zendō.

During his formative years as a Jesuit in Japan, Habito proved himself of high intellectual caliber by being admitted to the prestigious University of Tokyo, and acquitting himself honorably in its erudition. He successfully completed a master's degree and finished doctoral studies in Buddhist philosophy.

Ruben Habito is eminently equipped to write this book. I refer not only to his knowledge of Buddhism and Christianity and his practical experience of sitting in Zen, but more particularly to the phenomenon we have observed in the author of the deepening in his Zen practice resulting in the deepening of his social concern. He has introduced classes at Sophia University on the responsibility of the Japanese to their Southeast Asian neighbors, and he is a tireless worker in the Japanese Bishops' Council for Justice and Peace. His concern for his beloved Philippines is the constant companion to his grasp of the dynamic Oriental Emptiness.

Reading this manuscript, I am impressed by the way the author shows that our experiences in Zen are confirmed by the words of Jesus Christ as they are laid down in the gospel. It is also very valuable and gives a special flavor to this book that a true Zen Master, Yamada Kōun, who has a deep insight into Christianity, although he is not a Christian himself, not only gives a presentation of his own on the relationship between Christianity and Zen, but also takes part in a discussion with his Zen Christian disciples.

I am convinced that readers of this book will enjoy it and be helped to understand better the relation between Zen and Christian spirituality.

Hugo M. Enomiya-Lassalle, S.J.

Preface

I first heard most of the essays in this volume in the form of talks given by Ruben Habito to the members of the Zen Center for Oriental Spirituality in the Philippines. At the time, I experienced each talk as an encouragement to an authentic Zen practice and spirituality that does not take one away from social commitment, but deepens such commitment, making it whole and total. I trust that the publication of these essays will encourage others to realize that Zen does not stop at the inward journey. Rather, it begins from there, moving the practitioner to the discovery of a world where there is no more inward or outward, but where all merge and coincide. This realization enables the practitioner to plunge into a direct involvement with the heart of the human realities of suffering and pain, as well as the joys and hopes of the whole community. To enter such a world puts one thoroughly within the context of history, together with the whole of creation that struggles and groans along the path to Total Liberation.

It was not only Ruben Habito's words that helped us, but also his social concern and solidarity with our struggling people, especially the oppressed and the victims of injustice. I offer these words of appreciation also on behalf of the Ecumenical Association of Third World Theologians (EATWOT), recognizing that Habito writes out of a shared concern to integrate in concrete life the realities of faith and commitment, contemplation and action, dynamism and stillness, struggle and spirituality, wisdom and compassion, personal and social liberation. These realities are really expressions of one reality. But it is a reality that is not attained without struggle.

The Zen spirituality lived and expressed by Ruben Habito and others like him, the spirituality of commitment to integral human liberation that is valued and lived by us in EATWOT, and the spirituality in the midst of struggle that is lived and realized by so many of the poor of our world, are all the same. This understanding of spirituality was reflected in a statement issued by the Conference of Asian Bishops in 1978:

> Far from alienating us from sharing in human responsibility for the establishment of just and loving relationships among persons and groups in society, prayer commits us to true liberation of persons. It binds us to solidarity with the poor and the powerless, the marginalized and oppressed in our societies. It is prayer which brings us to the understanding of how injustice is rooted in the selfishness and sinfulness of human hearts. It is prayer which will help us to discern the tasks and deeds which can call on the Spirit to create within us both the courage and the love to bring about conversion in the hearts of persons and the renewal of societal structures.

In this spirituality of liberation, the twin call to dialogue of life with the poor, deprived, and oppressed multitudes, and dialogue with the great religious traditions of the people of Asia is being carried out not only on the level of words but especially in concrete experience. Thus this book challenges us to a total self-emptying and immersion among our people, contemplating and struggling, being one with the whole of creation, and living that others may have fullness of life and total liberation.

Sister Mary Rosario Battung, R.G.S.
EATWOT (Philippines) and
Zen Center for Oriental Spirituality

Introduction

The thought of putting this volume together came to me after a meeting with Sr. Virginia Fabella, M.M., of the Ecumenical Association of Third World Theologians, wherein she threw before me the following set of questions:

1. What is Zen all about?
2. What is its value and relevance for Christians?
3. What can its possible role be in God's liberating action in history?
4. Why do many Zen enthusiasts show lack of concern for issues of justice and social problems in general?
5. What is Zen's view of ultimate being, personal God, Christ, sacraments, etc.?
6. Can Zen have a positive contribution to an emerging Asian theology, taking into account two basic Asian realities; first, the poverty, exploitation and injustice under which many of our people live, and second, the multifaceted and profound religiosity of peoples in Asia?

These questions are loaded, to say the least, or perhaps better, explosive. They are asked by a Christian committed to her faith as well as to the struggle of all, especially Third World peoples, toward building a peaceful, more just and more human world. They are asked with an acute awareness of a world situation that is just the opposite of the above ideal, namely, a situation characterized by violence, structural as well as actual, by injustice, and by dehumanizing conditions that deprive millions of even the bare necessities of living. These conditions cry out for a fundamental reconstruction of the whole world socio-economic and political order, toward one that would enable countless human beings to lead decent human lives, or even more simply, one that would ensure the very survival of the earth itself, which is threatened under the present conditions.

Again the above questions are asked with a conviction that there is a liberating action operative in history upon which is based all Christian hope. It is the conviction that all this violence, all this injustice, all this dehumanization and destruction, which make us cry in anguish to the heavens — My God, my God, why have you forsaken me? — does not end in despair and defeat, but gives in to the reign of the Just One.

Likewise, the above questions are asked with an intent to bring out more fully the specifically Asian contribution to this liberating process, giving recognition to the Asian origins of Zen, coming as it did from India through China to Japan, and now to other countries including the Philippines.

The coming of Zen to the Philippines is particularly worthy of note in that it comes into a specifically Christian milieu; the majority of its increasing number of practitioners are faithful Christians, whether by choice and conviction or by mere force of upbringing and culture, or both combined. Yamada Kōun Rōshi, the Zen Master from Kamakura, Japan, who directed the first Zen retreat (*sesshin*) in the Philippines, is Buddhist, of course, but the person whom he has appointed to represent him first and to teach Zen in the Philippines is Sr. Elaine MacInnes, a Canadian religious sister of the congregation of Our Lady's Missionaries (O.L.M.), who was in Japan for a long time and finished *kōan* practice under his direction. Since then, there have been several Philippine-born Zen practitioners, both lay (Catholic) and religious, who have also finished the prescribed *kōan* practice under the same Yamada Rōshi and are likewise authorized by him to teach Zen.

Around Sister Elaine grew an ever increasing community of Zen practitioners from different walks of life — professionals, students, housewives, social activists, religious sisters, priests, and so on. Sister Elaine also found time to give regular Zen lessons to a group of political prisoners under the Marcos dictatorship while shuttling back and forth from Manila to the rural areas in Southern Leyte and Cebu, where she was also assigned to work by her congregation.

Incidentally, or perhaps quite naturally, a good number of this group doing Zen with Sister Elaine became deeply involved in the social movements that led to the now-historic Philippine People's Power Revolution of February 1986 and continue to be committed to the ongoing tasks that face their people and society. Many continue their grassroots work for justice and human rights; at least one has been appointed in the Cabinet of the Aquino government, while others go on in their respective ways of being involved in tasks of social change.

It is to this group in particular that the essays included in this volume were originally directed, either as informal talks or as prepared exhortations sent in absentia. I have been privileged to participate in several of their *sesshin* and to celebrate the Eucharist with them on such occasions through the years, and it is from them that I derived the challenge and inspiration to come up with whatever is presented here.

As I reread the essays, I find that the answers to the questions posed to me by Sister Virginia ooze out from between the lines; for example, the first two questions—What is Zen all about? What is its value and relevance for Christians?—are the very backdrop by which these essays came about.

The answer to the third question—What can Zen's role be in God's liberating action in history?—can emerge as one goes through a genuine experience of enlightenment, the very fulcrum of Zen itself, which liberates the person from ego-centeredness, toward a life emptied of selfishness and now lived in total freedom and in oneness with all beings. Such personal liberation can dispose the individual to see that the ego-centeredness that blinds and enslaves human beings has also contaminated the very socio-economic-political structures of our concrete world. This corporate ego-centeredness is seen now as ingrained and expanded into the social relations that make for oppression and exploitation and violence causing the misery of multitudes. True, the Zen experience by itself does not assure a socially-oriented vision that sees through the structural evils of society and calls for social involvement. What is called for is another step, which is the actual exposure to the realities of oppression and exploitation in being one with the sufferings of the oppressed and exploited in their concrete situations. Such an exposure, which draws forth the wellsprings of *com*-passion (suffering-with) that is the concomitant of the liberating wisdom of enlightenment, opens the social dimension in Zen and enables the individual to plunge himself or herself totally into God's liberating action in history, in all that this implies.

The fourth and rather insinuating question of Sister Virginia, as to why many Zen enthusiasts show lack of concern for problems of society and tend to concentrate only on themselves and their individual practice, may not apply to the persons described above, but it does apply to many others, whether in the Philippines or Japan or Europe or the United States, who may apparently be centering their lives on their Zen practice of sitting and "purifying their mind" in their daily lives, and stop at that. Zen practice, it is true, can serve as a form of escape into a world of contrived "peace and contentment" that is only a mask of that fundamental selfishness that is our mortal enemy. It can be another subtle form of spiritual hedonism, in search for a kind of inner satisfaction away from the turmoils of daily life. Or a person who may have at one time been engaged in tasks of social change can become "burnt out" or reach a near-hopeless state of ever running around in circles, and in a feeling of futility turn to Zen for solace.

In Japan Zen is recommended for and actually practiced by employees and executives of the big companies to ease their tensions and allay their frustrations, to enable them to go back with added vigor to their competitive and exploitative roles in society. Thus Zen is used as something that brings about a "catharsis" that diffuses conflicts and tames individuals, de-politicizing them and making them more malleable and more subservient to company interests. There are then insidious pitfalls that the practice of Zen as such is not immune from.

Treatments of the history of Zen beginning with meditative practices developed in India, introduced into and further developed in China and Korea, then transplanted to Japan, as chronicled by eminent scholars, tend to focus on the ascetical as well as the cultural elements, and with reason, as these are the most prominent and most celebrated aspects of Zen. And a cursory survey will indeed indicate that the social dimension is low on the priority scale of a great many who made a name for themselves in the history of Zen. We need not make excuses for this quite noticeable lacuna in fact.

The significant point for us here is to realize precisely that it is a lacuna, that is, something expected to be there but which is missing. And this is because the practice of Zen is a struggle with many stages, aimed at rooting out the fundamental self-centeredness in us that prevents us from seeing "things as they are." It is a long struggle that calls for an "inward turn," and unfortunately this inward turn, which is but an initial stage, can be so protracted as to engage one for years and years, before one is able to free oneself of inner shackles. We can perhaps regard this as a "novitiate" period where we need to cut out distracting social ties in order to devote our full energy to this task of self-liberation. Long hours of sitting practice, regulated discipline and deliberate detachment from certain social involvements are part of this "novitiate."

But it must not be forgotten that this prominently ascetic part of Zen practice is only an initial stage that is meant to be outgrown. Well-guided practice leads to its fruition in the experience of personal liberation in seeing one's true nature as empty. It leads to the attainment of wisdom, of seeing things as they are, without a tinge of ego-centered attachment. This very wisdom is the seat of compassion whereby the sufferings of all living beings become one's very own. And it is this identification with the suffering of concrete living beings in this very real world that is the firm basis of the at-one-ness and solidarity with the exploited and oppressed in their aspirations and struggles for a just and peaceful world, as we unite in a common endeavor to liberate ourselves from the violent and unjust structures of society.

One who has already plunged himself or herself into this struggle will find wellsprings of energy in the practice of Zen and will come to realize that every step in the struggle is rooted in self-emptying wisdom and compassion, in oneness with the joys and hopes, visions and aspirations of suffering living beings.

Sister Virginia's fifth question — What is Zen's view of ultimate being, personal God, Christ, sacraments, etc.? — can be misleading, as Zen is not so much concerned with theology or philosophy as with direct experience. The fundamental Zen experience is traced back to the Buddha himself, and this has been transmitted in the Buddhist tradition with its cultural presuppositions and verbal and conceptual apparatus. When a Christian goes into the practice of Zen and is able to enter into this experiential dimension as guided by a qualified Master, he or she does not necessarily forsake the Christian faith and assume a Buddhist set of beliefs. Rather, he or she is able to enter into the Holy of Holies where words and concepts fail, and where one can only stand in awe, humbled at one's nothingness and filled with gratitude for the blessing of this very existence. "Lord, it is good for us to be here," as Peter could only exclaim.

The realization of the centrality of this experiential dimension will put into proper perspective all talk about God, Ultimate Being, and so on, and will enable one to be no longer satisfied with mere words and concepts. As if one could fill one's hungry stomach by merely looking at a menu! No, God is no longer an idea or concept, but becomes real and factual in the concrete events of daily life. God becomes real in every breath, in every step, every gesture, in the smile of a child, in the rumblings of a hungry stomach, in the cries of anguish of a victim of torture.

As more and more persons enter into this experiential dimension offered by Zen, then the answer to the sixth question — Can Zen have a positive contribution to an emerging Asian theology? — will begin to work itself out. As one identifies with the situation of poverty and exploitation and oppression in which the majority of Asians are placed, and as one resonates with them in their particular religiosity, then the consequent human tasks in this light will make themselves evident. The actualization of this contribution toward an emerging "Asian theology" can be carried out precisely by those who have plunged themselves into these tasks and into God's liberating action in history.

It is hoped that this collection of essays will dispel certain misunderstandings about Zen, set it in better relief in its relationship to Christianity, and call greater attention to an aspect that has largely been left undeveloped in many treatments of Zen, that is, the social dimension, which is an essential feature of genuine enlightenment. The essays here have been originally delivered on or written for particular occasions over the past ten years, and hence are not organized as one systematic whole, although they have been revised for this volume. Hopefully they can serve as a menu that will invite readers to partake of the sumptuous banquet served us. And as one begins the meal, the menu must first be put aside, lest it get in the way.

1

Seeing into One's Nature

I was first introduced into Zen in the spring of 1971, less than a year after arriving in Japan from the Philippines, when a Japanese friend invited me to join a four-day Zen retreat (called *sesshin*, literally, "encounter of the heart") to be held at a Rinzai Monastery in Kita-Kamakura, near the Jesuit language school where I was staying. The four days of rigorous discipline—rising at 3:00 A.M., doing everything in strict silence broken only by warning bells and clappers and loud-voiced directives of the monk-assistants, time spent mainly just sitting in lotus position while paying attention to one's breathing—left me with aching legs and a back somewhat sore from the trainer-monks "encouragement stick" (called *keisaku* or *kyōsaku*, literally "warning device"), but it was for me a very powerful and exhilarating experience that whetted my appetite for more.

It was quite auspicious that my Jesuit spiritual director at the time had also been practicing Zen, and it was he who introduced me to the group directed by Yamada Kōun Rōshi at San-un Zendō in Kamakura.

At my initial interview or *dokusan* I presented my state of mind to the Rōshi, and he immediately gave me the famous *mu-kōan* to work on. This is the first in a series of *kōans* or "Zen puzzles" given to the Zen exercitant to aid in the practice of sitting, and to cut off delusive intellectualization. The *mu-kōan* begins thus: "A monk asked Jōshū in all earnestness: 'Has a dog Buddha nature or not?' Jōshū answered, '*Mu!*'" It was only a

1

couple of weeks after this that I was literally struck by a sudden earth-shaking flash of lightning while sitting quietly in my room, and I was filled with laughter and tears for several days afterward. Yamada Rōshi later confirmed the experience during *dokusan* as a genuine *kenshō* or enlightenment experience, as did his predecessor, Yasutani Hakuun Rōshi, who was visiting the Zen Hall at that time, in a separate interview. This marked my formal entry into the world of Zen. Nurtured by further *kōan* practice through the years, this same experience continues to inform all that I am today as it provides light for understanding the meaning of my Christian faith and of my whole existence.

How is one to describe this experience? All I can do at this point is to admit the futility of the endeavor, just as it would be futile to describe the taste of a cup of green tea or a chocolate bar. One can only point to a hot cup of tea and invite others to drink and taste it themselves. In the same way the gospel message itself is not a mere description of something but an invitation to "taste and see how good is the Lord." The words and concepts used to communicate this message at best serve an invitational function, that is, to a living encounter with the Lord "in the flesh."

In the inital instruction manuals for Zen practitioners, one is told of the "three goals of Zen." These are 1) the development of the power of concentration (*jōriki*), 2)attainment of enlightenment or awakening (*kenshō-godō*), and 3) the actualization of this Supreme Way of enlightenment in our everyday life (*mujōdō no taigen*). The discipline of sitting, paying attention to one's breathing, and so forth, naturally leads to the first goal, as one is able to "center" one's whole existence in the here and now of every breath, bringing together into one all the parts that tend to be disparate. The development of the power of concentration is a natural result of such disciplined attention and awareness, in sitting as well as in the activities of daily life. Thus one who undergoes the discipline and practices Zen sitting for a considerable period of time finds it a natural result to be integrated in one's life, "bringing the pieces together," so to speak, toward wholeness that is also wholesomeness.

But this integration and power of concentration is only an initial conditioning for what is really crucial in Zen, which is none other than the experience of enlightenment. And this is not achieved in a few hours of sitting, nor in a few months, nor even many years. In Christian terms this can only happen as a marvelous work of grace, toward which we simply dispose ourselves in our sitting practice, paying attention to our breathing, attuning ourselves to the here and now. Our human efforts do not *cause* the experience, but only enable us to dispose ourselves for that grace-filled event. Thus all the years of sitting and disciplined practice do not guarantee the "results" as such, for similar experiences can and do happen to individuals who have never formally sat in Zen at all. God in his total freedom can make children of Abraham from stones. Thus each person in his or her proper time is susceptible to that visit of grace; one can simply dispose oneself by attempting to remove as much as possible the human obstacles to it. And this is as much as the disciplined sitting and awareness can effect.

The occurrence of the grace-filled event is sometimes described in this way: The chick still enveloped in the eggshell attempts to wiggle out from within, removing crust after crust of the surrounding shell with its own little beak. Then, at the opportune time, the mother hen pecks the egg from the outside, and lo and behold, the shell is broken and the chick comes out into the light! The one timely peck of the mother hen is all we are waiting for as we try to wiggle out of our inordinate desires and basic ego-attachment by attempting to order our lives in the way of Zen discipline.

And once the shell is cracked, what is left is for the chick to continue the process of becoming a full-grown chicken. This third goal is also described as the personalization and appropriation of the enlightenment experience in our daily lives, enabling it to shed light on every nook and cranny of our day-to-day world. The breakthrough to the initial experience is like getting hold of a key to open the first *kōan*, and we find that it is a master-key that opens all the other doors as well! And now, further *kōan* practice is the attempt to actually use that key to open the other doors set before us in an exciting process of discovery that lets us go deeper and deeper into the mystery of the universe, and yet keeps us going back to where we have always been.

I must admit, though, to having had somewhat of a headstart with the Ignatian spiritual exercises that I was introduced to upon entry into the Society of Jesus. It was in the early sixties, during my novitiate days in the Philippines, that I had the privilege of undergoing the thirty-day Ignatian Exercises and was ushered into a way of life that included an hour of daily meditative silence and a yearly eight-day period of spiritual exercises in the Ignatian tradition. However, the way I was instructed in these Exercises tended to be rather cerebral, relying to a large extent on mental effort and theological fantasizing.

To be told in Zen to do away with conceptualizing and with mental effort and just to sit and pay attention to one's breathing was literally an opening of the windows of my being to let fresh air come in—the refreshing breeze of the Spirit of God which re-creates the earth and makes all things new. Theological ideas are but pictures, say, of a delicious piece of sweet dumpling, which may perhaps make the mouth water, but can never really fill the hungry stomach. Zen tells us to throw out the picture, grab the dumpling, open our mouth and take a bite.

To illustrate, I would like to refer to a Christian doctrinal formulation, namely the notion of "creation out of nothing" (*creatio ex nihilo*).

I was led to see the experiential significance of this "doctrine" with that initial experience in Zen precipitated by my working on the *kōan mu* presented to me in my initial interview with Yamada Rōshi: "A monk asked Jōshū in all earnestness: 'Has a dog Buddha nature or not?' Jōshū answered, '*Mu.*' "

At first I was inclined to do a bit of intellectualizing on this subject, having been trained in philosophy in my Jesuit formation, and also being of an inquisitive temperament. The original context of the *kōan*, of course, is simply a negative answer to the monk's question: No, dear monk, a dog does *not* have Buddha nature. But this goes against all of Buddhist doctrine, which affirms the Buddha nature (original, or "essential" nature) in all living beings, including dogs and cats, salamanders and cockroaches, etc. The *kōan* set me thinking about the concept of "nothing" or of "nothingness," and I started philosophizing about this notion.

But after reading Nishitani Keiji's *Religion and Nothingness,* I got the very important hint that this *mu*, which is so central and plays the important role of a fulcrum in Zen, is not the same as that concept of "nothingness" that is simply opposed to "being," but is something that transcends this dualism.

Working on this hint, I stopped my philosophizing, and I simply sat with my legs crossed, straightening my back, regulating my breathing, putting my whole being to focus on this *mu*, to become *one* with it, to be *absorbed (botsunyū =* literally, to lose oneself and enter) into it. *Mu* with every breath, every step, every smile, every movement. And it was this disposition that led to that explosive experience which was confirmed by the Rōshi, which now enlightens my whole being, and indeed enlightens the whole universe!

And so, our traditional Christian formulation of *creatio ex nihilo* is no longer for me a mere philosophical concept or doctrine that "once upon a time there was nothing, and then from thence came something," or whatever, but is simply an expression of an ever-present wonderment, with every breath, every step, every smile ... every leaf, every flower, every raindrop, realized as a grace-filled gift of God!

Everything in the whole universe, leaves, rocks, mountains, living beings of every sort, is simply and originally *nothing* but the gratuitous gift of God, uttered into being by His Word (Logos). Everything in its particularity is in a relationship of absolute dependence on the Infinite God, and nothing at all exists apart from this Infinite God. This can be expressed also in the phrases, "to live and exist in God, within God," and likewise, "to be enwrapped by the divinity." This is the foundation of the Christian view of the holiness of the whole universe.

To try to explain this with mere concepts or expressions based on philosophical thoughts and ideas, however profound, would miss the point. But as one is led to that experience of *tasting* God, one is led to taste one's nothingness in the face of God.

The Zen enlightenment experience is also called "seeing into one's (original) nature." For the Christian the image of this original nature is given to us by St. Paul as he writes to the Ephesians: "Blessed be the God and Father of our Lord Jesus Christ, who has blessed us in Christ with every spiritual blessing from on high, as he chose us in him before the foundation of the world, that we should be holy and blameless before him. He destined us in love to be his children through Jesus Christ, according to the purpose of his will, to the praise of his glorious grace which he freely bestowed on us in the Beloved." (Eph. 1:3-6). This timeless and boundless dimension of our "original nature" becomes vividly present in the here and now, and we are able to see clearly, as in another famous *kōan*, "without thinking of good or evil, one's original face, even before one's mother and father were born." (See *Mumon-kan*, a collection of Zen *kōans*, No. 23.)

With this enlightenment, words of scripture, which we tend to interpret intellectually or theologically, come back to us with a wondrous freshness and living presence. "The Kingdom of God is at hand!" (Mk. 1:15). To experience the Kingdom of God is to grasp in a very real way the coming of Christ, the becoming flesh of the Word of God. It is the very entry into the Christ-mystery, to partake in his death-resurrection (Rom. 6:3-4; Col. 2:12; Phil. 3:10; 1 Pet. 3:18-22, etc.). It is to die to one's old self, and to live in the newness of life in Christ (2 Cor. 5:15, 17). It is a newness of life (Rom. 6:4) whereby one no longer lives for oneself but in Christ, partaking of the life of God in him (Lk. 20:38). With this, one exclaims with Paul, truly, that "it is no longer I that live, but Christ in me!"(Gal. 2:20).

The experience of the mystery is an entry into a dimension that knows neither depths nor heights (Eph. 3:18-19; Col. 2:2-3; Rom. 11:33). After passing through the gateless gate of the initial enlightenment experience, the Zen practitioner is guided into further *kōan* practice by the Zen Master. This enables one to go on in fathoming these depths and scaling these heights, as one incarnates the mystery of Christ in one's concrete, everyday life. There is no thought, word, or action that does not become its concrete expression. Sitting, walking, drinking tea, doing menial tasks, washing one's face, looking at the stars, talking to a friend—everything becomes replete with *fullness* "in the Lord" precisely as one is *emptied* of oneself in every thought, word, action.

Every *kōan* is not meant to be an intellectual exercise, but is something to be "tasted and eaten." The *kōan* then is absorbed into my whole being, and I *become* the *kōan* itself, cutting through subject-object or self-other distinctions. The *kōan*, incidentally, may deal with a dog, a cat, a mountain, a star, a pound of flax, a person in distress, etc. Thus, Scripture passages can be seen as invitations to "taste and see how good is the Lord."

Living in this dimension, one realizes what it is to live as the body of Christ, given life by the same Breath of God: "So we, though many, are one body in Christ, and individually members one of another" (Rom. 12:5). This realization brings about tremendous implications for the social, cultural, political, economic and all other aspects of our lives. For now there is no one or nothing that is not an essential part of my very self. As the late Indian-born sage Krishnamurti put it, we are the totality of what the world is. And vice versa, the world is the totality of what we are.

As the pain in the little finger is felt by the whole body, I *cannot but* be concerned with what is going on in this world of ours, with all the pain, suffering and cries of anguish of so many living beings. They are *my* pain and my suffering.

Here may I just mention one element that I feel is quite distinctive for the Christian bent on the unreserved following of Christ: to contemplate on the life of Jesus of Nazareth is to assume this life as the archetype and model for one's own, and concretely this means taking the path he took, making the fundamental options he made his own. And this means to live one's life as totally opened to the Spirit (Breath) of God, in proclaiming the good news to the poor, in announcing release to the captives, recovering sight for those who cannot see, in setting at liberty the captive. (Lk. 4:18-19) This is a call for Christians to situate their lives with Jesus on the side of the poor, the oppressed of the earth, and to become an instrument for the proclamation of this good news of liberation.

The following of Jesus entails for Christians a definite perspective in looking at our present society, and that is from the standpoint of the poor and the oppressed, as bearers of the message of liberation that Jesus brought with his whole historical existence. It is this message that brought him into direct conflict with the religious and political authorities of his time, and that brought about his condemnation by those authorities and his death on the Cross. To follow Jesus is to place one's destiny together with the poor and the oppressed, proclaiming the message of liberation, and to accept the consequences of this message, as Jesus did. Of course, this includes not only the death to self, the death to all our ego-centered attachments, but also the manifold implications of such a death, in our concrete choices of our way of life, our values, our particular preferences in this historical existence. In the words of St. Ignatius of Loyola, "to be poor with Christ poor, to be despised with Christ despised."

The process of "emptying" in Zen disposes one to be perfectly free and able to place one's destiny with that of the poor and oppressed of humanity, whom one inevitably encounters in this historical existence, in the way that Kanzeon or the Bodhisattva Hearer of the Cries of the World becomes one with the sufferings of those she encounters, and offers a hand in the alleviation of those sufferings.

So to experience being "one in Christ" for the Christian involves not only a "general" or "universal" kind of oneness in eating and drinking and laughing and crying, but also a quite concrete kind of oneness with the sufferings of living beings in this historical existence, the oneness that Jesus the Christ himself realized as he assumed the sufferings of all humankind on the Cross. The contemplation of the Cross of Christ is then not just a self-flagellating or masochistic enterprise that relishes in the sight of suffering, but is a plunging of oneself into the lot of suffering humankind with Christ on the Cross. It is also a call to look at the very concrete ways in which living beings are made to suffer in our present day and age; to look at the poverty and hunger, at the destitution and deprivation, at the discrimination and oppression, at the various forms of military violence that desecrate the sacredness of human life, which is a gift of God.

To be one with this suffering and death of Christ on the Cross is also to be one with him in the newness of the life of the Resurrection: this solidarity with suffering humankind is the source of that energy that enables one to give oneself fully in the concrete historical tasks of liberation. Thus, the contemplation on the Risen Christ gives the vision that all this suffering is not in vain, that it does not all end in defeat and desperation, but in glorification and triumph. Right here, in the midst of apparent defeat and despair, is the vision of glory. It is on the Cross itself that Jesus tells the Good Thief, "Truly, today you are with me in Paradise." (Lk. 23:43)

To sum up, the life of Zen is not to be seen as a retreat into a world of passivity and euphoric contentment, but rather as a plunging of the total self into the very source of all life and action, here and now. Seeing into one's nature is seeing everything, each in its concreteness and particularity, as not apart from one's very own true self.

The Zen practice deriving from India and developed in China and Japan is historically situated within the Buddhist tradition, and thus the explanations of its orientation and goals, as well as the religious and ascetical elements associated with it, are presented in Buddhist terminology. But the Zen patriarchs and Masters themselves constantly emphasize the non-reliance on words and concepts, pointing directly to the experiential root of it all, toward the ineffable encounter of the heart. In exactly the same way, the words and theological concepts Christians are familiar with from scripture and from church traditions are but invitations to an encounter with the living God, who became flesh for our salvation. In this realm where the encounter takes place there is no longer Jew nor Greek, no slave nor freeman, no Buddhist nor Christian.

2

Zen Emptying and Fullness

"In a word, tell me, what is Zen to you?" asked someone who had heard that I had been doing Zen. Actually, the most apt answer would be, "Good evening," or "How's your wife today?" or "Let's have some coffee." Or even, "Well, . . ." Each word uttered, in its concreteness and irreducibility, is in itself fully the inexhaustible reality that Zen opens to all. Yet again, there is no word that can even approach this reality or *fact* of what Zen is all about. For words in the proper sense are merely pictures that can never fully capture what they aim to convey. This is something that must always be kept in mind in order not to be misled, especially in pursuing the series of words in the following pages.

But such an answer will leave many unsatisfied. Wishing to know Zen better, or to learn who they really are, or to discover ultimate reality, and so on, they earnestly seek some practical point to grasp so that they can travel the perilous journey that involves leg folding, and breath counting, or perhaps Mu-ing. They see this as a journey through darkness, rather arid and painful, especially for the legs and joints and back and shoulders, yet also refreshing, exhilarating, and for some, world- or universe-shaking.

So for those dissatisfied with the initial answer above, I ask forbearance in engaging in what can only be termed "dirty talk" in Zen, that is, words that rely on conceptual language, in the attempt to describe what basically can never be reduced to a concept. This kind of language only manages to hide the reality all the more from the seeker.

Given this caution, that the following utterances are merely faulty pictures and can never substitute for what they attempt to portray, let me answer the question above: "In a word, what is Zen to you?"

"It is . . ." I can stop here and say this is my answer, sit back and smile. And every Zen Master will return that smile, or perhaps chide me for a redundancy—but this would be repeating the same rigmarole above. And woe to the one who tries to interpret this "it is" as a statement about existence without attributes, just a simple "is," and so forth. No, I am not putting forth a metaphysical proposition. Here I would like to be practical and down-to-earth despite my temperament and background, which tend to leave me hopelessly up in the air at times. What I really want to answer is that, for me, *Zen is simply emptying*.

Now we have to get down to the tedious task of elaborating what I mean by this.

In our everyday lives we find our conscious selves "filled" with many things—memories of yesterday or yesteryear both bitter and sweet; plans for tomorrow or for the next vacation; thoughts about our daily tasks and menial jobs; grandiose projects, which would involve our time and energy; worries about our relationships with family; the demanding professor at school, the unappreciative boss at the office; worries about how we are going to make ends meet; worries about tomorrow's weather. Furthermore, mass media fill our thoughts with imagery both rich and trivial; the crime rate, the economic situation, this coming sports event, the movie that is the talk of the town, and so forth. All demand our attention.

As our conscious minds are filled with these things, which are normally unavoidable elements in our lives in the concrete everyday world, we at times get certain "twinges" that give us the forlorn feeling that living our lives "merely" on this level is shallow, superficial. Such feelings offer us a faint suggestion that there must be something more to life than all this. And so such "twinges from within" lead us to question the quality of our lives as lived merely on this superficial level of consciousness. They enable us to pose the question of whether there may not be a deeper dimension in ourselves undercutting this surface level that heretofore we have not been aware of, much less concerned with.

Asking such questions may lead some to pop-psychology books, which can occasionally offer us helpful insights about our lives in our relationships with others and in our emotional ups and downs, in our deepseated anxieties and insecurities, and in our need for affective support and adequate affective expression. Such books may also tell us of another level of consciousness to be explored, the "unconscious" wherein reside our dreams, our cherished hopes, our unexpressed reserves and conflicts. They may tell us how to overcome such conflicts, how to resolve such tensions within us, how to accept ourselves and accept others, and so on.

Now in all this we are enabled to see how both the conscious and unconscious levels of what we call our "self" are filled with so many things that leave us hanging in midair, that divide our existence into disparate elements that pull us in different directions, accentuating those conflicts we find within us. In all this we are enabled to see that what we are craving for, deep within, is a certain wholeness that would unite these disparate elements, a sense of wholeness that would in turn enable us to experience life as meaningful, worthwhile, joyful, beautiful.

Where are we to go in seeking this wholeness that our whole being craves?

Experience tell us that what we are looking for is not to be found by looking outside ourselves, in this or that pleasurable sensation, in this or that philosophical idea, however sublime, in this or that theological concept. Even if we turn to religion, and find there something that remains "outside" of us without touching the inner core, we will still be haunted by a certain hollowness. If we remain on this plane, that is, outside, we can never find the Source of our very self, from which alone that wholeness we are seeking can spring.

So what we are really seeking cannot be found by looking "outside." A line quoted by Master Mumon in the preface to his famous collection of *kōans* stresses that "Nothing which enters through the gate can be a genuine family treasure." He is saying nothing that comes to us "from the outside" can ever be counted as an heirloom to be cherished and passed on through the ages. And indeed our true treasure, the pearl of great price, is nothing apart from that which is hidden from the start in the field of our very own self. This is what we are called to dig up and bring to light. That wholeness that we are in search of comes from this very foundation, and so to get to that foundation means to delve into the depths of our own self—the only rock-bottom foundation upon which any solid structure can be built. And to do this means to undercut all the pseudo-structures that we have set up for ourselves, that are built upon sand.

It is these pseudo-structures that haunt us with that feeling of shallowness and superficiality mentioned above, that make us ill at ease with ourselves. This is the situation in which the Second Patriarch of Chinese Zen found himself at the beginning of his career; it led him to seek direction and become a disciple of Bodhidharma. A *kōan* from the *Mumon-kan* (No. 41) tells us of his search.

"Master, your disciple's mind is not at peace. I entreat you, set me at peace." Whereupon, Bodhidharma replies, "Bring your mind to me, and I will set it at peace."

The injunction of the Bodhidharma to the disciple is to no one but ourselves. Each and every one of us, in his or her own particular and unique temperament, is in earnest search for that same peace of mind.

Bodhidharma requires each one first of all to look within, look at the mind that is not at peace, fathom it at its very source, grapple with it, take possession of it, in order to be able to present it to the Master. The practice of this *kōan* involves that indefatigable search for one's own mind, with a plunging into the depths of oneself, and this is simply what we are doing in Zen sitting. In the course of this we are enabled to see in the proper light those things that we have falsely identified with our own self—our self-esteem, our social position, our security blankets, our material or even spiritual possessions, our natural talents and gifts, as well as our shortcomings, and weaknesses—all those things associated with our own self-image. We are able to recognize in a similar way those things that fill our mind "from the 'outside,'" that tend to divide us and set us into disparate elements. We are able to see through those and realize that the core of ourselves is one that is not contaminated by "outside elements." No, the True Self, the very mind we are required to take possession of, cuts through these elements one by one, getting to the core. This is similar to the process of peeling an onion whereby we take off and let go of layer after layer until we get to . . . what? Such a process is what I refer to in speaking about Zen.

The process can be rather trying, as we are forced to confront those pseudo-structures we have built for ourselves and toward which we nurture great attachment. We are called to peel them off one by one, to empty ourselves of them. This will give us a sense of not having anything left to cling to as we eliminate those things that gave us a sure footing, and with which we felt secure. No, the True Self is not this. And as we deepen in this process, going from one negation to the next—"neti, neti" (from the *Upanishads*, "not this, not this") what is left?

In the practice of the above *kōan*, the Zen Master plays a valuable role in pointing out those pseudo-structures, as we bring things to him that we have falsely identified with the mind. "No, not this. Go and search some more." This process takes a different amount of time or length of practice with each given individual. For some, it may take only a few weeks, and for some, several months. With others, it may require years and years. But it is only after having undergone such a process that one will be able really to grasp and make one's own that which the later part of the *kōan* conveys. The disciple finally comes up to the Bodhidharma and exclaims, "Master, I have undergone this process of searching for the mind, and I have experienced it as ultimately unattainable." It is only then that the reply of Bodhidharma directly rings in our very depths, and we know what he means when he addresses us, "I have finally thoroughly set it at peace for you."

Merely to read the *kōan* and try to interpret its content intellectually, without having undergone this taxing process of searching, mind grappling and emptying, is to miss its point. It is an invitation for us to enter this arduous process, the one we venture into every time we sit, composing ourselves by folding our legs and straightening our backs, regulating our breathing, focusing our minds to the point of ripe concentration. We are called to become the disciple himself, in his earnest search for peace of mind, in his indefatigable striving to get to the bottom of that mind and take possession of it, to experience the unattainable. It is there that a whole new world, a whole new universe, is waiting for us.

This invitation is no less than the one extended by Jesus to the rich young man in search of eternal life: "Go and sell all that you have, give it to the poor, and come, follow me."

Jesus was calling him to divest himself of all his cherished possessions, let them go, and enter a hitherto totally unknown territory in following the Son of Man — an act of total emptying of self, prerequisite to the full reception of the eternal life he was seeking. And entering into this realm is like entering through the eye of a needle, whereby all our excess baggage and attachments, false self-images, notions of self-importance, discriminative thoughts, and so forth, are recognized for what they are. They are merely hindrances we must cast away in order to attain what we seek.

To sit in Zen requires no less than a divesting of all our cherished possessions centered on the attachment to what we normally call the "self." We are called to undercut all the layers of this, to get to its very source and bring it to the Master that he may set it at peace. Actually, it is not so much the Master who sets it at peace from the outside, but the very discovery of that unattainable source, where it is, is itself the source of peace. And this source is eternal life. Eternal life is not that which we picture in our minds as something of endless duration, a mere extension of time that knows no end, or even a state of continued deathlessness. It is, rather, a realm that cuts through all our concepts of time, of birth and death, change and decay. It is a realm in which all our familiar concepts have run away, as all of them are limited by their opposites. Here in this realm, all opposites find their convergence, or coincidence, and the concepts as such are emptied of their content in being cancelled by their opposites. Here in this realm such notions as time and eternity, permanence and change, stillness and motion, universality and particularity, lose their force as opposites, that is, are emptied of content, and coincide. And such a coincidence (no mere coincidence, this) is not at all a concept but an event, a realm that waits to be experienced, as we submit to the process of emptying.

The new world into which Jesus invites the young man, which is the Kingdom of God itself, requires for its entry, this total self-emptying, which is, at the same time, a total self-giving and abandonment in trust. It is somewhat like that trust of Peter, when he jumped into the water at the beckoning of Jesus — it is a plunge like this that we are likewise called to take. It is only our own hesitations, second thoughts and calculating frames of mind, all indicative of a lack of trust, that cause us to bog down and sink.

This new world of the Kingdom of God that awaits us is an event, and attempting to describe it would be like trying to describe a bite of mango or a swig of San Miguel beer. Away with such attempts. All one can do is point and say, "Here it is, taste and see!" It is always here, right before us. Complaining that one cannot see it is like complaining of thirst when one is right in the midst of water, as an analogy of Zen Master Hakuin's famous poem brings out. Or to fail to see it as such is likened to the condition of a rich man's son who gets lost and wanders about a poverty-stricken village, unaware of his own riches, as the same poem illustrates.

So it would be entirely pointless to "describe" it as such. At best one can simply allude to it, to indicate its actual presence. That is also why scriptural references to the Kingdom are always of an allusive and illusive nature. They invite us to discover for ourselves the actual Presence. Lo, the Kingdom of God is in your midst! Taste and see that the Lord is good. It is something both hidden and revealed. It is not an idea or concept, but a fact to be grasped, felt, tasted. He who has eyes to see, ears to hear, let him see and hear!

To be able to see and hear in this way requires a total emptying, a casting away entirely of discriminatory thoughts that separate the seer and the seen, the hearer and the heard. No eye hath seen, no ear hath heard, the riches of the Kingdom! And this total emptying is on this very same account a total fulfilling of these riches.

"Emptying" is an expression of *process*, of *entrance* into the

Kingdom, from the point of view of *enlightenment as path*. From the point of view of *enlightenment as attained*, the term "emptiness" is most aptly employed. But a disadvantage of this term is that it is easily taken as a philosophical notion, which can sidetrack the Zen experience. Indeed emptiness, considered by some the central notion of Buddhist philosophy, is accompanied by a whole set of philosophical-metaphysical presuppositions, with implications for a particular outlook on the totality of reality. On the conceptual level this presents quite a formidable framework, as one understands by dabbling even a little bit in Mahayana dialectics. I am not talking of emptiness here as a philosophical notion in this context, but as an expression of the "content" (already a conceptual contradiction!) of an experience: "A clear blue sky, not even a speck of cloud to mar the gazing eye."

These two points of view in the Kingdom—entrance into it as process and the essence of it as attained—are represented by the complementary stances of the two disciples of the Fifth Chinese Zen Patriarch, Hung-jen (601-674). The story goes that the aging Hung-jen ordered his disciples to compose a stanza to show their inner states of enlightenment, so he could choose his successor from among them. The foremost disciple Shen-hsiu, (606-706) wrote:

The body is the Bodhi tree
The mind is a clear mirror stand
Strive to polish it always
Letting no speck of dust to cling.

Seeing this, a scullery boy working at the Zen monastery at the time wrote the following:

There is no Bodhi tree
There is no clear mirror stand
From the beginning not one thing is
Where then can a speck of dust cling?

This scullery boy, who exhibited his state of enlightenment through the stanza as handed down in the story, was then secretly chosen as successor and later became known as the Sixth Chinese Zen Patriarch, Hui-neng (638-713). Although these two stanzas are usually given as a contrast to emphasize the insight of the second, they can also be seen as complementary, giving us a fuller picture of the world of Zen.

The first stanza emphasizes the process whereby one maintains active vigilance in polishing the mirror of enlightenment, that is, the process of emptying as a continuing, ongoing event. The latter, on the other hand, emphasizes the state of being empty from the very start, and looks at everything from this standpoint, a state of perfect tranquillity. Although each already implies the other, their juxtaposition as complementary emphases serves to balance out the two elements of process and state.

Thus, the Kingdom is presented in scripture as calling for active vigilance, as in the parable of the ten virgins (Mt. 25:1-13) or in the eschatological writings. It is also presented as likened to a man who sowed seed and then went to sleep, with the seed growing forth on its own, independent of human effort (Mk. 4:26-29). Active vigilance is coupled with that passive stance of just letting the Kingdom "be," just like the lilies of the field and the birds of the air (Mt. 6:26-28).

In the two verses above the allusion to the mirror is pregnant. The enlightened mind is likened to a perfectly clear mirror. But there is no mirror as such, only what it reflects. And thus, the perfect clarity of the mirror, its total "emptiness," is precisely what gives it the capacity to contain the whole universe within it. The whole universe is perfectly contained in the perfectly clear mirror, as nothing stands in the way of things being fully reflected in it. Precisely because it is totally empty, it is totally full! Thus the fully enlightened mind, the fully emptied person, contains the universe in its fullness and totality, perfectly.

To understand better this likening of the fully emptied person to a perfectly clear mirror, a reference to the four characteristics of the wisdom of the mirrorlike, enlightened mind recounted in Indian Buddhist texts would be apt.

First, just as a fully polished, clear mirror of whatever physical size — from the tiny compact mirror to a large mirror the size of that in the reflector telescope at Mt. Palomar — is able to reflect everything totally, the mirrorlike enlightened mind is able to reflect the totality of the universe as it is. It is characterized by an all-embracingness that knows no bounds. Everything in the whole universe, in fullness and totality, is reflected in the mirror of the enlightened, fully emptied mind. Nothing is excluded from the realm of its concern. Indeed, only the fully emptied mind is able to comprehend, with all the saints, what is the breadth and length and height and depth of that which surpasses all knowledge. Only the mind that is totally emptied can be totally filled with all the fullness of God (Eph. 3:18-19).

Second, the perfectly clear mirror reflects all things in an equal way. It does not give preference to reflecting something because it is beautiful as opposed to something ugly, something large to something small, something colorful to something drab. All things are reflected equitably as they are. Thus the fully emptied person is able to accept all things and all persons as they are, in an equal way, without preference or prejudice, not choosing rich over poor, noble over lowly, attractive over ugly. Nor will such a person hold riches higher than poverty, attractiveness above ugliness. He or she will simply take these for what they are, as they are, without value judgment. In the Kingdom there is no distinction between "Greek and Jew, circumcised and uncircumcised barbarian, Scythian, slave or free" (Col. 3:11).

Third, while reflecting all things equally and equitably, without prejudicial stance, the mirror nevertheless reflects each thing and each person in its uniqueness, in its particular suchness. Thus something unsightly is as such unsightly, something beautiful is as such beautiful, hot is hot, cold is cold, black is black, gray is gray. In other words, nothing loses its particularity and irreplaceable uniqueness, each thing being what it is and uniquely so. In the Kingdom, though there is one body, the head is nevertheless the head, the ear is the ear, the eye is the eye. And likewise, the trunk, the arm, the legs, the foot, are each uniquely what they are.

Fourth, based on this particularity and uniqueness of each thing and person, the mirrorlike enlightened mind is able to respond to each in the manner appropriate in every circumstance. Fully emptied persons are able to give of themselves according to the particular demand or need that the situation presents. To someone hungry, they will provide food. To someone naked, they will offer clothing. To someone sick or lonely or downcast, they will be there for healing, to give solace, comfort, companionship, hope. In short, they are totally available and response-able to each situation, being "all things to everyone." "To the Jews, I became a Jew . . . to those under the law, I became as one under the law . . . to those outside the law, I became as one outside the law; to the weak, I became weak. . . . I have become all things to everyone" (1 Cor. 9:19-22). Such a universal availability, the capacity of being all things to all, is only possible to fully emptied persons, offering themselves totally without a taint of self-seeking or utilitarian motivation, in filling the needs of those around them. Such a person will be to others what they need him or her to be for them.

All-embracingness, acceptance of all in equality, recognition of each in its uniqueness, and universal availability and responsibility according to each one's needs—these are the four characteristics of the wisdom of the mirrorlike enlightened mind. They elucidate the inner state of the person who experiences that total emptying, which means entry into the Kingdom of God. Such a state, on the one hand, manifests full transparency, perfect tranquillity, "A clear blue sky, not even a speck of cloud to mar the gazing eye." On the other hand, it manifests the dynamic activity of everything reflected upon it—that never-ending activity of being born and growing and aging and dying.

What is to be experienced in Zen is characterized in such a way. It is therefore a misunderstanding to consider Zen an individualistic, self-centered practice or a solipsistic kind of spirituality. Such a misunderstanding is easily generated, even by those who practice Zen themselves, if they cut themselves off from the rest of society and its pressing problems. But that is a kind of spiritual luxury we cannot afford in a world facing tremendous socio-economic problems, a human society perpetrating various injustices in many subtle ways, a situation that calls for vigilant concern and active involvement for its betterment. Let us not retire into a haven of peaceful isolation in a quiet chapel where the cries of the rest of the world are drowned by the repetitious recitation of Mu or by the soothing sound of the air conditioner. Let us not think that Zen is merely that.

Heavens, no! If the Zen practitioner isolates himself or herself for a time in order to sit in stillness and find peace of mind, it is to look for his or her True Self, the discovery of which is the discovery of the real and deep bond that makes that person one with society, with the marketplace, with the whole universe.

Above I referred to the process of letting go of one's attachments, false self-images, prejudices and discriminating thoughts, and attaining that state of the "clear blue sky with no speck of cloud to mar the gazing eye," which is central in Zen. It is in the light of this clear blue sky that everything comes into right focus—the beauty of a rose, the smell of jasmine, the taste of porridge as well as the ache in one's legs, the noise of the speeding taxi, the dust on the road. Here one's True Self comes to the fore, in and through these things that make up the warp and woof of our daily existence. It is not something distinct from them. Here one is able to see one's True Self in the cry of a street vendor, in the hungry look of the undernourished child roaming the city sidewalks, in the plight of the displaced slum dwellers, in the pothole in the street that needs repair.

One who is fully emptied in Zen finds himself or herself in everything, literally, and is able to identify fully with everything, to be all things, and thus to act in total freedom, according to what the particular situation demands. Such a one is no longer separated by the illusory barrier between himself and the "other." One sees one's True Self in the "other," the "other" in one's True Self.

The isolation therefore that we choose in sitting in a quiet room for a time is something that ultimately leads to the discovery of our relationship with every being, not as an abstract principle or as a philosophical concept but as a concrete, factual event that is activated and makes itself felt with every movement, every gaze, every word, every touch. We choose such a period of isolation to sit in Zen in order to see through ourselves, to empty ourselves of everything that serves as a hindrance to the discovery of our oneness and solidarity with everything that is. So to realize this total emptying is to come to the realization of the infinite fullness in which we are one with the entire universe.

Yamada Rōshi likes to express this infinite fullness in emptying with a fraction that has zero for it denominator, as in 1/0, or 2/0, or 1000/0. The numerator in its unique particularity as a given sum is you and I, this tree or that cat, this mountain, that river, each concrete thing in the phenomenal world. The denominator expresses that point wherein emptiness is realized, True Self reached in total self-emptying. And as can be plainly seen, it is at this point precisely that infinity is reached. 1/0 equals infinity; similarly 2/0 or 1000/0 or one million/0 is also infinity. It is attained, grasped, in the unique particularity of each numerator, you and I, this mountain, this river. And from the standpoint of this *concrete infinity* (a conceptual absurdity) everything said above concerning the mirror begins to make sense.

A basic insight behind the formula *creatio ex nihilo,* "creation out of nothing," likewise hinges on this point. This is usually interpreted as a philosophical doctrine asserting the contingency of every being in its dependence on the Absolute God, Existence Itself, and so forth. Well and good. But rather than taking it as a philosophical doctrine, we can take it as an invitation to that experience of the nothingness that is at the heart of our being, which becomes the fulcrum for experiencing the infinite life of God in us.

This experience of the infinity of God in us, which is also the experience of our nothingness, propels us to the concrete uniqueness that is our self, putting our feet back to touch the ground, or better, our posterior on the *zafu* (sitting cushion) and from there to the same concreteness of our standing and walking, laughing and crying, eating and drinking, going to school or to work, digging ditches or filling street holes, building bridges — to the concreteness of each act or each passivity that is a complete and perfect manifestation of the Infinite.

The "Ultimate Reality" reached in Zen, then, is nothing separate from each and everything we do, or are, in our everyday life, in the concrete. This is illustrated very well by the *kōan* in which a monk approaches Master Jōshū (of the *mu-kōan* fame) and says, "I have just entered the monastery. Please instruct me (in the essence of Zen)." To this Jōshū asks in return, "Have you had your breakfast?" The monk answers, "Yes, I have," whereupon Jōshū tells him "Then wash your bowls." And at this, the monk attains a flash of insight into the essence of Zen (Mumon-kan, No. 7).

The insight attained by the monk in this case is not some abstruse philosophical truth about Zen, or even some profound Zen doctrine interpreting the "meaning" of Jōshū's words. No. It is nothing apart from his having taken breakfast and washed his bowls.

On the nature of this insight, Mumon's poem exclaims:

Because it is so very clear
It takes longer to arrive at the realization.
If you know at an instant that candlelight is fire
The meal has long been cooked.

Indeed it is so very clear, clearer than the blue sky. What is clearer than having breakfast and washing one's bowls? Sitting and standing, walking and running, getting tired, feeling warm, wiping the sweat off one's face?

The essence of Zen is nothing more than simply having one's breakfast, washing one's bowls. To use some more "dirty" language to becloud the issue, it is to become full, in realizing one's True Self as one with the whole universe. Or again it is to empty oneself of such ideas or thoughts of realization and self, and universe, and to simply be one-self, one's True Self, in the daily tasks of living, rising, taking breakfast, washing up, going to work, getting tired, resting a bit, meeting friends, saying goodbye, getting sick, growing old, dying. Yet this is not a conception of rising, taking breakfast, washing, and so on, but *just that*, doing, replete with a fullness that excludes nothing—a *wholeness*, wherein one's whole being is in that act of rising, or taking breakfast, washing, or whatever. Each act or passivity is, in being totally empty, fully and perfectly a manifestation of the True Self.

The ultimate goal of Zen is nothing more, and nothing less, than becoming truly what one is: truly human, whole, at peace, at one with everything, yet emptied of everything. Such an ultimate goal is not outside the reach of anyone; the Kingdom of God is at hand, in our midst. He who hath eyes to see, let him see. . . . But to be able to see requires that total change of heart, *metanoia*, that total emptying of self that makes for its true fullness. Zen Master Dōgen's famous line on the Way of the Enlightened points to this very experience: "To attain the Way of the Enlightened is to attain one's True Self. To attain one's True Self is to forget oneself. To forget oneself is to realize one's unity with the whole universe."

The great death to self is the birth to the newness of life, wherein birth and death will be no more: "Neither shall there be mourning nor crying nor pain, for the former things have passed away" (Rev. 21:4). And what remains? A new heaven and a new earth, transparent in the clear blue sky, in which everything is "filled with all the fullness of God" (Eph. 3:19). But these are mere words, hollow, clanging cymbals, unless one actually, bodily goes though that experiential path of total self-emptying in which lies this fullness. Zen opens this experiential path to anyone who cares to tread it.

3

The *Heart Sūtra* on Liberating Wisdom

Zen halls and temples in Japan often resound with the chanting of the *Heart Sūtra*, a well-known piece of Buddhist scripture, highly regarded as a succinct expression of "the essence of enlightenment." However, it must not be forgotten that Zen does not rely on verbal or conceptual expressions for the transmission of the essence, which is none other than the living wisdom of enlightenment. Words and concepts are in Zen like a finger pointing to the moon, and it would indeed be foolish to be so enthralled with the finger, gazing at it, analyzing it from various angles, making comparisons with other fingers, as to miss the point, that is, the moon in its resplendent brilliance. Let us then look at the *Heart Sūtra* as a finger that points to the moon. Look, how radiant!

The "heart of the matter" that the *sūtra* is concerned with is *prajñā-pāramitā*, which I translate freely as "liberating wisdom." *Pāramitā* means the "highest, perfect, supreme." It also means "gone beyond (to the other shore)," "transcendent," characterizing the wisdom (*prajñā*) of one who has attained liberation from "this shore," this world of conflict and suffering. However, it must be stressed that this liberating wisdom *does not make one cease to be in the midst of this world of suffering and conflict.* No, one does not thereby cease to be human, as one continues to face the ordinary (and extraordinary) struggles that are part and

25

parcel of humanity's lot. But the person who has come to this liberating wisdom finds perfect peace and freedom right in the midst of this life! This does not mean that he or she relishes the suffering or conflict, or that he or she has simply taken a passive stance that tolerates it, doing nothing to prevent or stop it. What is meant is that liberating wisdom enables the enlightened person to transcend all opposites such as suffering vs. comfort, conflict vs. harmony, good vs. evil, life vs. death, this world vs. the other world. Liberating wisdom fully accepts each situation each moment in its eternal fullness, be it in sickness or health, riches or poverty, success or failure, life or death, and as such overcomes these oppositions. It is perfect freedom in perfect acceptance!

Liberating wisdom makes the person at peace with himself or herself and with the whole universe, one with all, truly free, truly happy, truly human. It is the fount of genuine compassion whereby one's heart embraces all, where one is united with all living beings in their joys and sufferings, struggles and hopes. This wisdom lies latent in all of us, and its awakening will enable us to realize our life in its infinite fullness, in every particularity, as one awakens in the morning, takes breakfast, goes to work, relaxes, chats with friends, wipes off one's sweat, laughs, cries, sits, stands, falls asleep. In this wisdom one is perfectly free, in perfectly being what one is, just as one is.

Let us now take a look at the *Heart Sūtra's* account of this wisdom.

1. THE BODHISATTVA AVALOKITEŚVARA

The sūtra opens with Bodhisattva Avalokiteśvara (*Kuan-Yin* in Chinese) in the practice of the profound *prajñā-pāramitā*, going on to describe what he (she) perceived in this practice.

First of all, the term *bodhisattva* (literally, "wisdom-seeking being") refers to one in active search for this liberating wisdom. It was applied first to Gautama himself, referring primarily to the six-year period of religious search and discipline he underwent before attaining supreme enlightenment. In undertaking this search he left a life of comfort and ease and security at the royal palace and immersed himself directly into the mystery of human suffering.

The term later took on other nuances, a prominent one being the seeker-after-wisdom who, in the final stage of the search, just before entering *nirvāṇa*, chooses to remain here for a while in order to help and guide other living beings in their search. There are several bodhisattvas of popular devotion mentioned in Buddhist scriptures, and our Avalokiteśvara is among them. The name means one who perceives (hears and sees) the cries of suffering of all living beings in an unhampered way. In the Japanese pronunciation of the Chinese translation, this is *Kanzeon* or *Kannon Bosatsu*, and has come down in feminized form as a goddess who hears the cries of distress of all suffering beings. She is portrayed as having innumerable hands and faces, signifying her ability to see in all directions, bridging all distances, and to extend whatever form of assistance each suffering being needs in his or her particular situation.

This readiness to hear the cries of the suffering of others and to extend a hand of assistance in their direction is thus to be understood likewise as the inner attitude of every seeker-after-wisdom. Such an inner attitude is further expressed in the fourfold vow of the bodhisattva, likewise recited regularly in Zen halls all over Japan and elsewhere.

> *Living beings are innumerable — I vow to save them all.*
> *Illusive desires and lusts are inexhaustible — I vow to*
> *extinguish them all.*
> *Gates to the Truth* (Dharma) *are numberless — I vow to*
> *learn and master them all.*
> *The Way of the Enlightened is peerless — I vow to realize*
> *it.*

By this vow, the bodhisattva embraces the whole universe, opens his or her heart to all beings in their service, and sets out to accomplish the "impossible dream, to reach the unreachable star." Likewise, by this it becomes clear that the search after true wisdom does *not* involve a self-centered kind of religious discipline whereby one closes off the world and other people from one's concerns to lead a life of escape, seeking only one's own peace of mind, avoiding involvement with a troublesome world and troublesome people. One sits in *zazen* not as an isolated individual, but with the weight of one who bears the whole universe, who has embraced all living beings.

To give a noted example of a bodhisattva in our century, let me mention Miyazawa Kenji (1896-1933), a devout Buddhist who spent the latter part of his short life (he did not live to be forty) living and working among poor farmers in Northern Japan. His inner attitude is summed up in his short poem entitled "Ame ni mo Makezu" (Undaunted by the Rain), a part of which goes as follows:

> *If in the East a sick child be,*
>   *Rush to his bedside, attending to his need.*
> *If in the West a weary mother be,*
>   *Go, carry her bundle of grain for her.*
> *If in the South a dying man should lie,*
>   *Go and comfort him, saying "Fear Not."*
> *If in the North a quarrel ensues,*
>   *Go and say "Stop such foolishness."*

These words reveal a readiness to be of service where needed, like the hands of *Kannon Bosatsu*, ready to be extended to anyone in need.

Another example that comes to mind of an unflagging religious search coupled with perfect openness in the service of others is the life of Simone Weil. Her diaries and journals published after her death reveal to us a heart as wide as the universe, having made her own the sufferings of all the unfortunate who have ever lived, having lived in her body the pain of all the afflicted.

The bodhisattva is seen in contrast to the complacent, unreflecting person who nonchalantly leads his life in the pursuits of the senses and in the gratification of selfish desires. He has begun to see the futility and emptiness of such pursuits and has begun the search for something deeper, something lasting, for a "treasure that will not rot and no thief can take away" (Cf. Lk. 12:33). But the seeker does not thereby become a recluse who has abandoned this world in favor of another world, the "spiritual" in which one can find one's own peace and comfort. To do so would simply be to shift the level of pursuit to another plane, the "spiritual," and would be a mere continuation of a basically selfish orientation, the opposition of "this world" to "the other (transcendent) world."

The true search for liberating wisdom is not a way of abandonment that turns one's back on the real world, the world of conflict and suffering, but a way of *embracing acceptance* that plunges the seeker right into the midst of that world precisely in order to conquer it. In Christian terminology, the royal road to the kingdom of heaven is the "way of the cross," whereby one follows Jesus in embracing the reality of human suffering and in so doing accomplishes the salvation of the universe. The fact that the *Heart Sūtra* sets forth the Bodhisattva Avalokiteśvara as the realizer of liberating wisdom, as the model of every seeker, is quite significant in this respect. The seeker must *become* Avalokiteśvara himself (herself), hearer of the cries of suffering of all living beings. Thus is the path of realization of liberating wisdom opened.

2. PERCEPTION OF EMPTINESS

"When the Bodhisattva Avalokiteśvara engaged upon the practice of the profound liberating wisdom, he (she) perceived that the five constituents of existence are devoid of substance (empty)."

In the Buddhist conceptual framework, human existence is analyzed by way of a set of five constituents, namely, 1) matter or physical substance (*rūpa* in Sanskrit, often translated vaguely as "form"), 2) sensation, 3) perception, 4) volition, and 5) consciousness. We shall not trouble ourselves with an explanation of these categories, but shall simply rephrase the statement of the *Heart Sūtra*: everything we consider as constitutive of our existence (in whatever way the elements are conceived to be, upon detailed analysis) is "devoid of substance" (*avabhāva-śūnyam*).

The first temptation is to wax profound in a philosophical interpretation of this statement, which is rather crucial for the understanding of the whole of Mahāyāna Buddhism. However,

we are not concerned with an intellectual appreciation of
Buddhist doctrine, but rather with the living realization of wisdom as such, which can shed light on the question of our own
existence. And to be told that what basically constitutes our
existence is "devoid of substance" is like having the rug pulled
out from under our feet, overturning whatever common sense
we have about the substantiality of this existence of ours. In
short, this statement of the *Heart Sūtra* presents a challenge to
our common sense and accepted ways of thinking, introducing
a contradiction in our assumptions, like a sharp sword that
lunges directly at one's heart, cutting right through one's most
cherished conceptions. It is to be told that whatever one con-
siders "substance" is "devoid of substance."

A mind-boggling proposition indeed, being told that "A is not
A." This is not unlike the famous *mu-kōan* in which to the question, "Does a dog have Buddha-nature?" Jōshū answers *mu!*
And now the practitioner is asked by the Master, "What is *mu*?
Show me *mu!*" As a practitioner goes forth to present one answer after another, he is told, time and again, "No, not this!"
After a while, he is driven into a corner, having exhausted all
conceivable answers. Then his conceptual thinking comes to a
full stop as he faces a blank wall. It is only in this full stop, this
zero point of conceptual thinking, that there can burst forth the
liberating power of *mu*, unleashing all the energy of the whole
universe, re-creating everything anew.

It is only from this standpoint of the full stop, *zero point,* that
one can grasp the full import of the term "devoidness of substance" or "emptiness," that is, after one has actually gone
through the process. Hence there is no use in waxing profound
on a theory of "the meaning of emptiness" and the like, as it
will only seem to provide another conceptual alley that will actually block one's coming to that full stop. Thus the seeker now
must gear himself or herself toward that full stop, and "devoid"
himself or herself of everything that comes in the way. How is
this to be accomplished?

The way consists in divesting oneself of everything—that
process of *emptying* that I have already dealt with. And now the
Heart Sūtra offers an additional hint in this process. It urges the
throwing away of that view of our existence as "substantial," in

other words, that clinging to what we may call the "phenomenal self" or "ego," the root of all selfishness and avarice and envy and lust and what-have-you. It is this clinging that sets a human being in conflict with another, that alienates a person from others, from nature, from his or her own True Self; this is what must be emptied.

It is my clinging to this phenomenal self that makes me want this car, that house, more money, the admiration of others, the power to influence people's lives, a name to be remembered in history. My pursuit of these things sets me in conflict with others who are also after them. Here we have Juan and Pedro each wanting a larger and larger share of cake, being at odds with one another, Juan grabbing Pedro's share, Pedro getting even through physical violence, Juan retaliating, and so on — the world of opposition and conflict, and mutual exploitation among human beings, as their self-interests are set against those of others. On a global scale we have ethnic group against ethnic group, nation against nation, rich nation exploiting poor nation, poor nations seeking to get the better of each other, resulting in mutual resentment and often physical warfare. A bird's-eye view of the world today presents such a picture of conflict everywhere, and this is nothing but the extension of that attachment to the phenomenal self that is deeply rooted in each individual.

The rightful understanding of what the *Heart Sūtra* means by "devoid of substance," or "emptiness," then, involves the letting go of this phenomenal self or ego, a total emptying, which is no less than a complete abandonment of all of one's cherished possessions — not unlike the call received by the rich young man who was in search of eternal life (Mk. 10:21).

So the central statement of the *Heart Sūtra* that "the (five) constituents of existence are devoid of substance," is the *fundamental negation* not only of our whole conceptual apparatus, whether we think in line with the Buddhist conceptual framework or not , but primarily of our ego-centered existence. Our ego-centered existence is "devoid of substance" — empty. This negation is thus an injunction to divest ourselves of such a mode of existence. It is a call from a self-centered life, unreflective, engaged only in the pursuits of the senses and in the gratification of selfish desires, to a life lived in the search for an eternal treasure, in the search for that liberating wisdom that opens the heart to others, the call to walk the path of the bodhisattva. For a life of self-centeredness, life lived in the pursuit of the desires of the phenomenal ego, can only end in frustration and futility. Such a life is like a structure built upon sand, a structure bound to crumble from the very start.

And where is the secure foundation for the new edifice to be found? Where is the fount of that lasting treasure, liberating wisdom? It is on the experiential arrival at *zero point* mentioned above, whereby one grasps indeed that *all is emptiness*, and *emptiness is all*! A clear blue sky, with no trace of cloud to mar the gazing eye.

One is opened into an entirely new world, and yet nothing changes of the old: mountains are high, valleys are low, roses are red, violets are blue (or some shade of indigo). I wake up in the morning, take breakfast, go to work, rest a little, joke with friends, drink when thirsty, fan myself when hot, shiver in the cold. And yet again all this is seen in an entirely new light: each of these particularities is a full and perfect manifestation of that world of emptiness, each action and passion replete with a fullness of its own, each moment an eternity.

That experiential *zero point* is the fulcrum on which is based the liberating wisdom that the *Heart Sūtra* speaks of. And at this point all opposites are reconciled, as the universe of concepts gives way to the universe of living experience.

3. NEGATION OF CONCEPTS — INVITATION TO DIRECT EXPERIENCE

"Here Śāriputra, all things are of the nature of emptiness. They neither arise nor are annihilated; they are neither stained nor unstained; they neither increase nor decrease." We are faced here with more conceptual contradictions, and our common sense understanding of things is shattered. How are we, for example, to reconcile the above negations with the everyday facts that babies are born, people die, things get dirty, they are washed clean, the population increases while the food supply decreases, and so on?

I will tell you a secret. There is no way to reconcile these in

our heads. It is just that everything seen from *zero point* is *just as it is*, without any concepts of "arising" or "annihilation," of "impurity" or "increase," and *then* we can see indeed that there is no arising nor annihilation, no purity nor impurity, no increase nor decrease. A baby is born, and cries "Uha!" *Just that.* A famous actress dies of cancer at the age of seventy-four. *Just that.* Oops, that passing car splashed all this mud all over my white shirt and trousers. *Just that.* Ah, a single wash with soap brings back the whiteness. *Just that.* I must have lost half-a-kilo in the past week with all those wearisome meetings. *Just that.*

We can now get a hint as to the next string of negations that the *Heart Sūtra* confronts us with. The five constituents of existence (mentioned above) are negated. And so are the organs of sense, their respective object-fields, and the various sensations that result from their functioning. And likewise the twelve links in the chain of causation, beginning with "ignorance" and ending with "old age and death," together with the Four Noble Truths, and finally, the doctrine of enlightenment itself. In other words, all the basic teachings of Buddhism are here negated.

For a pious Buddhist, all this must be tantamount to blasphemy, denying outright what has been traditionally revered as the teaching of the Buddha himself. It is as if a Christian were to deny the doctrines of the Apostle's Creed one by one. I am reminded of another "blasphemy," frequently repeated in Zen, whereby one is enjoined, "If you meet the Buddha, slay him!" One is tempted to say to the Christians, "If you meet the Christ, crucify him!"

Such injunctions are indeed jarring, even shocking, but they are willfully so, and with a purpose. For "doctrines" and "holy images" can become an additional set of encumbrances that prevent one from the direct realization of what they were originally meant to convey.

Buddhism itself began with a powerful religious experience — that momentous experience of enlightenment of Gautama, which totally altered his outlook and his whole personality. It was a dynamic experience, which continued to inspire his whole career and affected those who came in contact with him directly or indirectly. Buddhist doctrines came to be formulated mainly as attempts to verbalize, conceptualize, and systematize that experience (a futile attempt from the start!) for the purpose of transmission to others. But the mastery of the verbalized, conceptualized, systematized teaching does not necessarily accompany the grasp of the essential point, which is the experience of that enlightenment, the fount of liberating wisdom. On the contrary, such verbalization, conceptualization and systematization can positively hamper this liberating wisdom from coming to the fore.

The function of doctrines in Buddhism has frequently been likened to that of a raft: it can indeed be useful in carrying one over the waters, but to continue to carry the raft even after getting ashore would be to shoulder a useless burden. But here in the *Heart Sūtra* the raft is abandoned even in midstream; it is the only way to discover that what one is looking for, what one is aiming at right from the start, is right here *in the midst of the water!*

Thus the injunction to kill the Buddha if one meets him along the road is the command to do away with one's mental images of the Buddha, as well as to do away with the opposition of "Buddha" and "non-Buddha" or "ordinary being." With the image thus eliminated, the real thing comes to the fore, and then one is able to see everything with the eyes of the Buddha himself, with the eye of nondiscrimination that has transcended all such opposition.

The parallel injunction to the Christian about "crucifying Christ" may have a different ring, but its purport is the same — to clear away all our pious images of Christ and thus "put him in his place," which is on the cross, where he is one with all beings in their suffering, where he is reduced to nothing in total emptying (*kenosis*, Phil. 2:7). It is this total emptying on the cross that leads to the bursting forth of the new life of the resurrection, that is the salvation of the whole universe. And for the Christian, this is not merely a past event that happened some two thousand years ago to some wandering Galilean, but it is a present reality here and now. The basis of the Christian life is this cross and resurrection, total self-emptying and total newness of life. We are not concerned here with a "theology of the cross," but with a direct experience of a present reality. "It is no longer I that live, but Christ in me" (Gal. 2:20); Christ crucified and resurrected in the newness of life, empowered with full authority in the whole universe.

The negation of doctrines and concepts is neither agnosticism nor intellectual anarchy, but an invitation to experience the reality that underlies the doctrines and concepts.

To give another example, the denial of the doctrines of God's existence is usually interpreted as the acceptance of an atheistic worldview. But this is itself the setting up of the opposite *doctrine* of God's nonexistence. Liberating wisdom would *deny* both, presenting the invitation to experience the reality of God *as is*, in the clicking of this typewriter, in the music from the tape recorder, in the buzzing mosquito, in the cherry tree outside the window. It is the invitation to see everything in the very eyes of God, *as is*. O blasphemy of blasphemies, yet wonder of wonders: "everything is filled with the fullness of God!" (Eph. 3:19). "Every time I hear a newborn baby cry, or touch a leaf, or see the sky. . . ."

But again, let this not be mistaken for pantheism, the doctrine that equates everything with God. There is *no doctrine here*, but simply an invitation to hear with the ears and see with the eyes of the heart: the clicking of this typewriter, the music from the tape recorder, the buzzing mosquito, the cherry tree outside the window. "Blessed are the pure of heart, for they shall see God" (Mt. 5:8). This is the vision available only from *zero point* as mentioned above. A clear blue sky, without a trace of cloud to mar the gazing eye!

4. THE TRUTH OF SUFFERING

Among the Buddhist doctrines the *Heart Sūtra* sets up for negation are the Four Noble Truths, the Truth of Suffering, the accompanying Truths of the Cause of Suffering, the Cessation of Suffering, and the Path to the Cessation of Suffering. The Truth of Suffering expresses a rather fundamental feature of our human existence, and its negation in the *Heart Sūtra* again forces us against a wall.

Gautama embarked on his religious journey in quest of the key to the mystery of human suffering. Jesus crowned his short earthly career by fully accepting intense suffering and an ignom-

inious death upon the cross. Suffering is a blatant fact I encounter, in varying degrees of intensity, in my day-to-day life.
Even a surface awareness of the situation of the world today
puts one face-to-face with this fact. Hundreds of thousands
throughout the world live on the brink of starvation and in constant threat of death; numberless refugees are either still on the
high seas or facing an uncertain future in poorly equipped ref-
ugee camps; millions in Asia, Africa and Latin America are
deprived of even the bare necessities of human existence due to
flagrantly unjust social structures; millions of industrial laborers
in various countries are constantly plagued by oppressive working conditions and unfair labor practices, treated as mere tools
of profit rather than as human persons; countless individuals
and groups throughout the world are discriminated against or
persecuted for their race, religion, skin color, sex, political con-
victions, and so on. It is indeed an endless list.

The underlying presupposition in all this is that suffering is
an undesirable element that humanity strives to eradicate from
its existence with all the means at its disposal, and that the
picture of an ideal existence would be one freed from such suffering. Hence, we tend to make distinctions between this world
of suffering, this "vale of tears," and the "other world," "the
other shore" where all such suffering has ceased, where all is
bliss, whether it be the Buddhist *nirvāṇa*, the Christian heaven,
or some form of earthly utopia. The attainment of such a state
is the hope that springs eternal in the human heart.

How then are we to take the negation of the Truth of Suffering in the *Heart Sūtra*, which states that "there is no suffering,
no cause, no cessation, no path to the cessation of suffering"?
What does this mean to the father of the family of eight whose
shanty has just been demolished by government troopers to
make way for the construction of a hotel and tourist center? Or
to a young couple who have heard from the doctor that their
first child of less than one year is dying of a skin disease aggra-
vated by malnutrition? Or to a political detainee who is subjected to interrogation and physical abuse at the hands of the
military, deprived of needed sleep, food and drink?

A glimpse of an answer came to me recently during a meeting
with a group of farmers and their families in a barrio in the

northern part of the Philippines. A few weeks before, ten of their companions had been picked up by military troopers and, after being abused and tortured, were sent home, except for three, whose bodies were found burnt to the bone upon exhumation from a common grave in the cemetery of the next town. And now the bereaved families and some sympathetic friends were gathered together at this meeting, reporting further developments and consulting with each other as to what steps to take. For it seemed that the harassment by the military would keep on, as they would come to the farmers' homes fully armed in search of certain family members who in turn were forced to go into hiding; in the meantime the soldiers would prey on whatever they found available—chickens, livestock, and so forth.

It would be too complicated to describe fully the background of the situation, but this group of farmers and their families were being forced to the edge of a cliff. Should they turn in the family members who were being sought by the authorities? Some of these were girls in their teens, and their fate could well be imagined if they were to fall into the hands of the soldiers. The people knew if they kept on refusing and maintaining them in hiding then there would be no end to this present harassment. In the meantime they could not go back to work on their farms as long as this situation continued, and thus their very source of life was being threatened. In other words, given the alternatives, there was no conceivable way out for them. They were faced with a living *kōan*, a *kōan* with the weight of life and death.

This living *kōan* is precisely what led them to *zero point*. And what happened at that meeting I was privileged to attend was a communal experience of *zero point*. Their lives had been emptied of all possible human hope, and they had, literally, nothing more to lose. And it was in this situation, emptied of everything, that everyone felt a new freedom, a new light. The way one of them expressed it to me was, "God is with us now. We have nothing to fear!" And this expression uttered right then was not a mere "hope" or "faith" but an *experienced reality* that showed itself in the serenity of their faces, in the lightheartedness that came to that very moment. "God is with us now. There is nothing to fear!"

The above description does no justice to the actual experience of the meeting itself, of a group placed in the very midst of physical and mental anguish and persecution, facing basic dilemmas in which there was no conceivable way out, accepting themselves as such, and experiencing something which liberated them from such suffering *while being right in the midst of it* — a human experience of something close to pure joy and freedom and peace, right in the face of their contraries. *Zero point.*

I do not know what happened to the members of the group afterward. Some more may have been picked up by the military, perhaps even killed. Some may still be in hiding. Some may still be . . . some may have already . . . I do not know. All I know is that whatever happened afterward, "God is with us now. There is nothing to fear!"

Let us not be held back by attempts to "analyze" or "interpret" this expression, which for them came spontaneously from a deeply felt Christian conviction. Let us simply open our inner eye to see it from within, from *zero point*. It is from this same *zero point* that the *Heart Sūtra* exclaims, "There is no suffering, no cause of suffering, no cessation of suffering, no path to the cessation of suffering."

5. NO WISDOM, NO ATTAINMENT

Another puzzling statement of the *Heart Sūtra* appears, which seems to subvert everthing the very *sūtra* stands for: "There is no wisdom, no attainment." We are again placed in apparent self-contradiction, after all this talk of liberating wisdom and the ways to its attainment.

Let us recall, however, that this is uttered from the standpoint of that wisdom itself, shining in full splendor as the noonday light. On a bright, clear and cloudless day, the pure white light of the sun illuminates all things and lets them be seen just as they are. It is the pure white light that enables everything to be seen, yet it itself does not come within vision. In the same way, liberating wisdom, while enlightening all things and enabling everything to be seen as it is, itself does not come within the field of vision; it is oblivious of its own existence!

This "obliviousness of its own existence" is what makes for the total freedom and detachment of liberating wisdom. It betrays no "self-consciousness" that sets up an opposition between itself as "wise" and something else as "foolish." This oblivious- ness and total absence of self-consciousness is what makes the person matured in liberating wisdom hard to notice in a crowd. There is no sheen, no glare, no flashy element that would attract attention to itself.

In Zen one who comes to a certain experience of enlighten- ment sees an entirely new world for the first time, and for a time remains in the thrall of the novelty, the wonderment, the brilliance of this new perspective. In this immediate stage after that experience a certain glare remains, a certain consciousness that goes with the powerful emotions that the experience may have triggered. A tinge of attachment to the "enlightenment experience" remains, understandably, because it is something very intimate, very precious, something that has definitely af- fected his or her entire outlook on life and on the universe. But if this gets out of hand, it easily leads to what is known as "Zen sickness," overenthusiasm with Zenlike expressions and para- phernalia, coupled with an extra normal propensity to bring Zen into normal conversations even when uncalled for, an overzeal- ousness to "convert" others to Zen. Or perhaps worse, one un- wittingly succumbs to the temptation of pride, because "one has had an experience which others have not," and in unsubtle ways one begins to flaunt that fact.

But such a pitfall is alien to genuine liberating wisdom. It is the task of post-enlightenment training to grind away this sheen, to sweep away this self-conscious attachment to the experience, and to enable the practitioner to become his or her normal self again, reacting as a normal being in all things, seeking food when hungry, rest when tired, heat when cold, feeling indignation against injustice, compassion for the suffering of others. And yet again with a difference. In each of these events and encounters in daily life, the person is one with his or her True Self, one with the entire universe. Each event, each encounter exhausts one's total self, and there remains an infinity to give. Each mo- ment is a complete realization of the True Self in each concrete situation. But in all this, there is no need to think twice and say, "In this act I am one with the universe." No, one is simply so, and that is all.

In the same way as liberating wisdom is oblivious of its own existence, true compassion, which springs from it, is characterized by the total absence of self-consciousness. The truly compassionate person spontaneously becomes one with another in suffering. He or she does not have to pause and say, "Ah, what a pity!" as if from the standpoint of one outside the pain. One is spontaneously able to make that pain one's very own, and thus respond accordingly *from within* the pain itself. A mother nursing her sick child does not have to say to herself, "Ah, poor child, suffering in pain." For the pain of the child is her very own pain, and she feels the pain perhaps even more than the child itself and is entirely oblivious to her own discomfort in giving the child the care it needs in its sickness.

Thus true compassion does not count its "merits" and feel complacent at having done a "good deed." For example, in the New Testament injunction to the man who has two coats, that he give one to him who has none, the giver will have no room to say to himself, "Ah, I did a good thing in giving him that other coat of mine; I expect at least a sense of gratitude from him (the wretch!)." For he has simply done what is most natural in the situation, as water would flow from a higher to a lower place, without the least feeling of condescension. In true compassion based on liberating wisdom, the left hand knows not what the right hand is doing (Mt. 6:5).

At this point I am reminded of the story of two Zen monks, a young man and his elder companion, riding on a crowded train on their way back to Kamakura after an errand in Tokyo. The young monk was at all efforts to keep a posture becoming of a monk, careful and wary of the gaze of the other passengers. The elder one, on the other hand, looked tired and kept nodding his head in half-sleep while standing and holding the suspended leather strap for balance. When they reached the station, the young monk half-chided the elder for being so carefree, letting others witness such a sluggish and lazy-looking old monk. At this the elder monk in turn retorted, "Be your natural self and do not strive to parade your virtue before others. Was it not your self-consciousness that became your attachment and separated you from the others? The truly wise man does not concern himself with exhibiting his wisdom."

It is only when one is firmly grounded in liberating wisdom that one can truly, freely say, "There is no wisdom." From the same standpoint one can say, "There is no attainment." For what is there to attain for one who dwells at the highest of attainments? Or from another angle, liberating wisdom simply comes to the fore, as clouds of delusion that block the pure white light disappear. This is no attainment, but simply a coming to what has been right there from the start. And as the clouds of delusion caused by our self-centered thinking fall off or thin out, the seeker is freed of all hindrance of mind, and hence of fear and anxiety. Having shed all delusive attachments, he or she has nothing more to lose, nothing more to gain. One is simply *as one is*! What peace of mind, what freedom, what exhilarating joy! This is *nirvāṇa*, the highest enlightenment (*anuttarasamyak-sambodhi*) in which all the Buddhas of the past, present and future dwell.

6. CONCLUSION: THE *HEART SŪTRA* AS MANTRA

The last few lines of the *sūtra* extol its glories as a great, vivid, unsurpassed and supreme *mantra*, and end with a Sanskrit formula of the *mantra*. This word originally meant a phrase or formula to be kept in mind and recited repeatedly in order to set the mind of the religious practitioner at focus on one point. The meaning further developed as a formula with dynamic power able to effect the union of the reciter with all the power in the whole universe. Thus the recitation of the *Heart Sūtra* itself is believed to effect the realization of enlightenment in the very recitation, in the way Christian sacraments are understood to have the power to effect what they intend, which is union with God, in their very performance.

In the light of the above, seeing that the exposition of liberating wisdom is the be-all and end-all of the *Heart Sūtra*, such belief is not entirely without grounds. The whole *Heart Sūtra* itself, as we mentioned in the beginning, is like a finger that points us to the moon, shining in all its brilliance on a cloudless night. So the earnest recitation of *Heart Sūtra* can become a trigger for that experience of enlightenment. But again, it does not have to be the *Heart Sūtra*. The sound of a gong, the ticking of a clock, a sneeze, the smile of a friend . . . a dewdrop, a whisper, a gentle breeze. Look, how radiant!

4

Kōan: Every Day
Is a Good Day

The sixth entry of the *Pi-yen-lu* or *Blue Cliff Records* collection of *kōans* begins with a question posed by Master Yün-men: "I am not asking you about the previous fifteen days. Now say something about these latter fifteen days."

The concrete reference of the *kōan*, first of all, is to the waxing moon (first fifteen days) and the waning moon (the latter fifteen days). The break-off point here is the full moon or the experience of *kenshō* or self-realization. Thus, the "previous fifteen days" refer to the period before enlightenment, a period of searching and digging and delving and "Mu-ing," wherein one applies total effort to enable the True Self to come to full light.

The "latter fifteen days" begin with and presuppose the experience of enlightenment. That experience is the discovery of one's True Self as one with all, as being no different from each and every particularity in the whole universe. This is the experience of the "full moon" of one's life. Indeed, in this experience, replete with joy and peace and inner satisfaction, one sees the *concrete* meaning of one's existence, not as an intellectual idea, but as a down-to-earth *fact*. With this one becomes fully at peace and at home with oneself and the whole universe, and one is content even in the face of death. For the enlightened person, and for that person alone, every day truly *is* a good day. The point of the *kōan* is to show one's realization of this "good day." "Now let your servant depart in peace, because my eyes have seen your salvation." The words of the prophet Simeon in Luke 2:29-32 reflect this kind of joy and sense of fulfillment at having come to what one has awaited and longed for over a long and arduous period. I am reminded of other words which have somehow become a part of me: "And now my own joy is made complete" (Jn. 3:30).

Though varying with each individual, this experience of the "full moon" is so fraught with emotional overtones and undertones that it can take time for the sheen and luster to settle. A misdirected step can afflict one with what is usually called "Zen sickness," in which one keeps referring to this experience even out of context or keeps throwing around Zen terms and phrases in conversations, even when they are not called for. One can come close to being a Zen maniac, trying to convert everybody in sight to this "very wonderful thing." Indeed, Zen may have done wonders for one, but for the bystander or onlooker or unfortunate victim of Zen talk it may simply be a smack of the exotic. The Latin term for moon is *luna*, the root of the word *lunatic*.

A mere hairbreadth distance from this, however, is the healthy Zen path, which calls for further unflagging exercise in polishing and rounding off the rough edges. The post-*kenshō* *kōan* training is thus a vital element and can make for the subtle difference between a pathological and a healthy Zen mind.

If we go back to the moon analogy, we see that the latter fifteen days is in the direction of a return to total darkness of the "new moon." It is a period of shedding attachment to the *kenshō* experience as such, culminating at that point wherein sheen and luster are no more, and one is completely lost in the midst of darkness, that is, in the naked reality of this concrete day-to-day existence. Of course, now there is a great difference, a crucial difference, from before the experience of the full moon. Now one is at peace, at home with oneself and with the totality of the universe, no longer worried about perpetuating one's name or honor or riches or self-image. One is simply *there*, with every breath, every cough, every step, every event, every encounter, to the full.

It is about these "latter fifteen days" that Master Yün-men is asking. And he himself answers his own question.

EVERY DAY IS A GOOD DAY

It is easy to mistake this answer and think that Master Yün-men means every day things turn out just fine. Let us not be misled by the words here though. Master Yün-men is speaking from the depths of the "essential world," *de profundis*, and not talking about phenomenal events.

Similar language is found in the Book of Genesis, when God created the waters and the earth and plants and animals and human beings: God looked over the whole universe of his creation, each and every thing in it, and saw that *it was very good*. A total and unconditional affirmation of each and everything as it is.

Again, this expression is not dealing with phenomenal events, or with goodness or badness of things in the phenomenal world. It is this dichotomy in words that leads to such questions as, If God created everything and saw that it was very good, why are there so many evils in the world? Innocent babies dying of disease and starvation, innocent people brutally murdered or subjected to military harassment, small elite classes enriching themselves at the expense of the worsening poverty of the multitudes. And so on. Indeed, we live in a world full of contradictions, full of evil and suffering and injustice. Does Master Yün-men close his eyes to these realities?

No, *not at all*. In fact, if you work on this *kōan* in the *dokusan* room and present a situation wherein everyday is fine weather, things going smoothly, business growing, everybody happy, and so on, you will be sent back to look at the *real* world, to present an answer based on *that*.

To be able to utter "Every day is a good day," from the true standpoint of the essential world, one must have a solid grasp of the world as it is, and not some imaginary utopian kind of world where it never rains and there is only sunshine, like southern California.

Let us take a stark look at this world of ours to be able to grasp the true import of Master Yün-men's words.

Recently I received news about a former college classmate who was killed by the military in a rural area in the Philippines. He had been "underground" for many years, having lost all hope for change through the conventional, legal and political means. I remember back in college days how he had been an active student leader, full of hope, full of concern for his country and his people. A tragic end for someone who had given his life for Filipinos in the way his conscience dictated.

And he has not been the only one either. Countless others are losing their lives in a similar manner when voicing the injustices being perpetrated in our society, in this real world of ours today. How about the labor leaders, male and female, whose only concern is to serve their fellow laborers in organizing for solidarity, so that they can stand up for their rights and be treated as human beings? They have found themselves branded as subversives, and have now either been arrested or subjected to continuing harassment.

The local scene already makes our hearts heavy with the sufferings of our own people, and the international scene is not bright either. The slaughter of hundreds of innocent Palestinian refugees in Beirut a few years ago sent shock waves into our hearts. And there is the continuing political violence in El Salvador, Guatemala and other Central American and South American countries whose peoples have been bearing the yoke of exploitation for hundreds of years. And that is not to mention Cambodia, or Afghanistan, or even the similarly complicated problems in different countries of the African continent.

How do things look for the future? The report to the Club of Rome entitled *Limits to Growth* does not paint a rosy picture. Nor does the *Global 2000 Report to the President—Entering the Twenty-First Century*, by the Commission on Environment and the U.S. Department of State. These and other reports about the future *indicate* (not merely predict nor foretell, but statistically project, based on present situation and trends) that by the year 2000 about 80 percent of the total population will be living in the Third World, and the number of those living below the poverty line will drastically increase. At present, of five billion inhabitants of our planet, 850 million are living in a situation of absolute poverty and starvation, and are on the brink of death.

It is estimated that every minute, twenty-seven persons die of starvation-linked causes on this earth of ours. At the very moment this is being read, in different places all over the world, such deaths are occurring one after another. And by the year 2000 the estimated population will be from 6.3 to 6.8 billion. And of course the number of starvation-linked deaths will keep on rising. Countless innocent individuals will be deprived of their basic rights to live by a situation of injustice and an unbalanced distribution of the world's resources and means of production.

Another impending reality that causes concern for humankind now is the continuing destruction of our natural environment. The earth's natural resources are being depleted by rampant and thoughtless exploitation in order to support the luxurious consumer habits of those who have money and power, at the expense of those who do not. One indicator of the situation is that by the year 2020 practically every available rainforest resource in the Third World will have been depleted if the felling and destruction continues at the present rate. It is estimated that in Asia alone the forest area decreases by one million eight hundred thousand hectares per year. And all this is not yet to speak of environmental destruction from other causes, such as pollution due to large-scale industrial projects, or from nuclear-caused radiation, all of which are growing on a global scale.

And still another impending concern is, of course, the militarization of our globe, which includes the continued "development" and stockpiling of nuclear weapons. The present stock is already sufficient to blow up the earth several times over, and yet we continue to create and store these destructive weapons. It is estimated that the military expense of all countries of the world combined is close to two million U.S. dollars *per minute*. Besides nuclear weapons, of course, conventional weapons are continually being manufactured and sold to authoritarian and repressive regimes to check the rising voices of discontent among the people.

Such are the contradictions of our real world today. This situation reminds us of the Burning House Parable in the famous Mahayana scripture, the *Lotus Sūtra*. The Buddha, depicted as the compassionate Father of all beings, looks at the world situation and compares it to a house whose walls and posts are burning and are about to collapse. His children remain oblivious of this fact and continue to romp and play inside the house, unaware of the coming destruction.

This is the real world that we are called to stare in the face before we can go on to tackle Master Yün-men's *kōan*.

But a hint into this *kōan* is also given to us by an entry in the *Miscellaneous Kōans After Kenshō*, concerning the stone in the bottom of the Sea of Ise:

> *In the sea of Ise*
> *Ten thousand feet down, lies a single stone.*
> *I wish to pick up that stone*
> *Without wetting my hands.*

Let me not dally with an explanation of this *kōan* as such, but simply mention the continuing part of the *kōan*, which tells us that *that* mysterious stone both "cannot get wet" and yet also "cannot get dry." These two apparent contradictory characteristics of *that* stone, which we can call the stone of the Essential Nature of our True Self, give us the hint for grasping Master Yün-men's "Every day is a good day." "Cannot get wet" means that there is absolutely no opposition in this world, no object to be made wet or subject to wet with, or the other way around. There is no polarity between subject and object, being born and dying, happiness and sorrow, good and evil. "Cannot get dry" means that tears of compassion continually flow in this concrete world where living beings are in a state of suffering. And both these characteristics of this "mysterious stone" describe the situation seen from the point of view of the essential world as such.

I recall the words of a wise man from India who said, "What you are, the world is." And to this we have to add, "What the world is, is what you are." This is to see things in a way that dissolves the opposition between ourselves and the "world." The "world" is "what we are." The world is not something outside of us, something that we view as mere bystanders, lamenting its sorrows and evils. No, what happens to the whole world as such is what happens to our very own True Selves. The sickness of the world is our very own sickness. This is the sickness of the bodhisattva; it is a sickness that is also the hope and salvation of all living beings. In Christian terms it is the cross of Christ, the bearer of the sufferings of the world.

It is only the truly crucified who can say with Master Yün-men, "Every day is a good day."

5

The Song of Zen

All beings are originally Buddhas.
As in the case of water and ice,
There is no ice without water,
No Buddhas apart from living beings.

Not realizing that Truth is so close,
Beings seek it far away—alas!
It is like one who, while being in the midst of water,
Cries out for thirst.
It is like the son of a rich man
Who gets lost in a poor village.

The reason why beings transmigrate through the six realms
Is because they are lost in the darkness of ignorance.
Wandering about from darkness to darkness
How can they be freed from the circle of birth and death?

As to the Zen of the Great Vehicle,
No amount of praise can exhaust its treasures.
The six Ways to perfection, beginning with Giving,
Living a right life, and other good deeds,
Intoning the name of Buddha, Repentance, and so on,
All these come down to the merit of Zen sitting.
The merit of one single sitting in Zen
Obliterates countless sins of the past.

Where then are the evil ways that can mislead us?
The Pure Land cannot be far away.

Those who, even once, with a humble disposition
Are able to hear this Truth,
Praise it and faithfully adhere to it,
Will be endowed with innumerable merits.
But if you turn your gaze within
And attest to the Truth of essential nature,
That Self-Nature that is no-nature,
You will have gone beyond mere sophistry.

The gate of oneness of cause and effect is thrown open.
The path of non-duality, non-threefoldness right ahead,
Form being the form of no-form,
Going and coming back is right where you are.
Thought is the thought of no-thought.
Singing and dancing are the voice of Truth.

How boundless and free is the sky of samādhi.
How refreshingly bright, the moon of the Fourfold Wisdom.
At this moment, what is it you seek?
Nirvāṇa is right here before you.
Pure Land is right here.
This body, the Body of the Buddha.

(Zazen Wasan or *Song of Zen*
by Master Hakuin, 1685-1768)

This song can be heard in Japanese Rinzai Zen halls, and so it should be helpful for us to try to grasp it, although not intellectually, of course. Let us try to get a sense of its background so that we will be able to taste it. Let us always be wary of the way we receive Zen teaching, which is like a finger pointing to the moon. When someone says, "Look!" let us not stare at the finger, but become aware of the brightness of the moon, which enables us "to see." Let us listen not to the words, but to the voice within.

Hakuin Zenji was a famous and prominent Japanese Zen monk who lived during the Tokugawa period. He is called the second founder of Zen in Japan, because during his time, due to sectarianism and petty rivalries, Zen was coming to the point of degeneration. Hakuin became the living manifestation of Zen life and thus served as a teacher by example. He entered the Buddhist monastery at 15, and early in life was well-acquainted with the basic problems and harsh realities of life and living. At 24 he had his *kenshō* approved. He had been doing *yaza* (night sitting) and as he heard the temple bell "gong," everything was released.

For Hakuin it was the sound of a temple bell. For Shākyamuni the twinkle of the morning star triggered the experience that revolutionized his universe. It also revolutionized the world, because that experience started a great movement, which still influences us in a very profound way. We are, of course, influenced by many movements. We can see this not only in Buddhism but in Christianity, too. We are a melting pot in history where many influences are able to dialogue with one another. We are able to partake of this from our given wholeness, our given definiteness, from what we are, here and now. And now, we are called to a similar experience, that experience which revolutionizes the universe!

Wasan means "praise," so Hakuin was singing a song of praise to Zen. It was a song of acclamation: "How beautiful! How lovely!" This is not an intellectual expression but an exclamation of an inner state. In reciting this song of an inner state, we are invited to go into that inner state within ourselves. This is the way to chant the *Zazen Wasan* by Hakuin Zenji. It must be sung as a background to our very own sitting experience, our own search for that True Self.

When he was 33 years old, Hakuin went back to his home and became caretaker of his father's temple. At that time the districts in Japan were divided into jurisdictions of the various Buddhist temples, as part of the plan of the Tokugawa regime to unify the people. Everyone had to register at a given temple in his or her area, rather like the parish system in the Catholic church. And so, from the time he was 33 until his death at the age of 80, Hakuin was a simple country parish priest, so to speak.

That life embodied in itself the fullness of the Zen life in the concrete. He accepted things as they happened and responded very simply without any calculation. It was as a simple country temple priest that he was able to occasion a wide revival of Zen all over Japan. He did not write great tomes, but he had a grasp of the abstruse doctrines of Zen and occasionally wrote treatises concerning some of them. One of his achievements is the Song of Zen. Hakuin Zenji was a very practical man, concerned with the poor and sick in his parish. He was knowledgeable about all kinds of illnesses and knew how to mix special herbs for certain diseases. He was also famous for his calligraphy. He was gifted in many respects, and, with it all, he remained what he was, a simple country temple priest!

As Shibayama Rōshi points out, the *Wasan* divides naturally into three parts. From the first line to the line "How can they be freed from the circle of birth and death?" is a kind of introduction, which gives the presupposition of Zen, and states for us the way things are. It tells us about the universe and how we are meant to experience it. "All beings by nature are Buddha" puts the theme in Buddhist terminology. We Christians would perhaps say, "All things are permeated by Divine Nature." But let us not be attached to words. Let us see what the words point to in our own experience and in our understanding of ourselves.

The second division begins with the acclamation, "As to the Zen of the Great Vehicle" and ends "how refreshingly bright, the moon of the Fourfold Wisdom." This section is the heart of the text. It mentions and explains many Buddhist terms and several other points that require an understanding of Buddhist background. This section gives us the essence of Zen, which is not doctrine but experience, the presupposition of which is found in part one. The second part tells us what we are meant to experience and contains primarily a thrust toward experience.

The third division comprises the last four lines and is a kind of summary that presents the way to actualization. The whole song is summed up in the last few words, "This body, the Body of the Buddha." In a nutshell we can say that that is our purpose, to try to grasp and taste what those words stand for, "This body, the Body of the Buddha."

SONG OF ZEN, PART I

The opening presupposition is "All beings are originally Buddha," or "All beings are primarily Buddha." We Christians say, "All things are permeated with Divine Nature." This is an attempt to express the truth of the whole universe, the truth of what we are. This realization is not the exclusive property of any sect or religious group, and it liberates us from our own sectarianism in the way we consider Zen. The truth that we experience is not the property of only Zen Buddhism as such. In the same way we say that the universal truth that Catholicism attempts to present is not the *exclusive* property of Catholics. The word *catholic* is *kat'holos* and means "of the whole." So to say "All things are permeated with Divine Nature" is an expression of something that is meant for all, a universal truth.

We cannot deny that sometimes one way of expressing a truth is clearer than another. Also, there are certain ways of expressing it that enable one to appreciate it more. Although we really do not have to do Zen in order to get at or experience that truth, we may find Zen a shortcut in attaining the experience of truth.

It is not only because you are sitting in Zen that you come to *kenshō*. Nor is it automatic that if you do Zen you will possess the truth. Neither is it only by human effort that it comes to us. To experience truth deeply is a great gift. It is also at the same time a catharsis that prevents us from being attached to Zen itself. Yamada Rōshi always warns us about "Zen sickness"... because we value our Zen experience, we try to talk other people into it. Doing this brings about the opposite effect. Instead of unifying us with others, it blocks our relationships, because we come to be identified, for example, as "Zen enthusiasts" out to "propagate" Zen to others.

What is the universal truth? How are we to attain it? The truth of Zen is something that can be grasped only by concrete experience. Christianity is a parallel. It is not a set of doctrines but rather an experience, a call to enter the Kingdom. "The Kingdom of God is at hand.... Open your ears to accept the good news." What is the good news? Simply that "All beings are permeated with Divine Nature ... open your heart to that reality." This is basically what we do when we sit in Zen. We are preparing ourselves for that conversion, transformation, the metanoia required of us if we are to enter the Kingdom of Heaven . . . the Kingdom whereby we see that all beings are permeated with Divine Nature . . . all beings by nature are Buddhas.

This is the sense of the first line of the *Song of Zen*. All the Zen practices and *sesshin* are our frail human attempts to prepare ourselves to receive that reality. What are the things we do? We straighten our posture, regulate our breathing, and unify our minds to concentration — con-centric . . . going to the center.

Ordinarily in our daily lives we are dispersed or separate; appointments here and there . . . fragmented moments in time . . . disparate efforts . . . never attaining wholeness. Our Zen discipline gears us toward a wholeness by first unifying our selves. The power that arises from sitting is *jōriki* and with it we become our integral selves through the practice of posture, breathing and concentration.

In becoming whole we are able to present that whole self. We then see it as it is. We present ourselves as whole, and we become the bread and wine we offer at Mass . . . something whole and one!

Whole and complete and one and perfect as we are, we are also incomplete in our step-by-step personalization of this reality. This is the contradiction we find in the *kōan* about the various stages of the Zen road. There is no end to the attainment that one can realize. One has to go further. There is always a higher step than the one attained. We are called to become infinitely more complete and perfect. So when we say we are complete and perfect, it does not mean that we can stop there. We are still called to another step toward perfection. Saint Ignatius expressed it in his words with the term *maior*; our perfection is not a static state where we can rest. Something that gives us peace and joy calls for more!

We have a kind of basic understanding of God . . . an infinite "Deus semper maior" — God always transcending himself in his infinity. That is dynamic growth, always perfect and complete, yet still going further toward greater completion. It sounds like a contradiction, but that is the only way we can express it. To attain this is what we attempt in our sitting.

To be whole and to become more and more whole ... the opposite is to be dispersed, separate, every few minutes doing something else, being somewhere else. But our whole lives can be permeated with wholeness, whereby every moment we are totally and completely in *this* moment, here and now. And this moment is not anything removed from the previous complete moment. It is another culmination of all that we are. It is toward this wholeness we are moving as we make every step. "All things are permeated with Divine Nature."

To summarize, this *Song of Zen* is an acclamation based on the inner state of the Zen life. It is something that emanates from the kind of living that is Zen life. We are called to enter that world ourselves, and as we sing or recite this song, perhaps we can get a taste of what that world is all about. Let us continue in that growth toward wholeness, in that growth or entry into the world in which we are all one, that world in which all things are permeated by Divine Nature.

SONG OF ZEN, PART II

In our introduction we spent some time tasting the opening line. Now I would like to reiterate the first line, "All beings are originally Buddhas." In Genesis we read that God looked at all of creation, at each and every single creature, and God saw that it was all good. The goodness is its participation in the Divine Nature, which permeates everything. This fact should not remain in our heads; we should become deeply aware that the goodness is simply what we are trying to experience in Zen, and in that goodness we participate in the infinite goodness of God.

In Japanese the first sentence is "*Shujō honrai hotoke nari.*" The word *hotoke* in Japanese is somehow synonymous with the divine, the sacred, the good. In lauds we praise, "Bless the Lord, all you earth and sun and moon and plants and birds of the air." How can the sun say, "Bless the Lord"? It does not have a mouth! How can a flower say, "Bless the Lord"? More to the point, how can *we* bless the Lord?

"The permeation of all things by Divine Nature" is open to misinterpretation. It might be thought of as a doctrine of pantheistic. Some Christians are afraid of Zen because it seems to be pantheism. But there is no doctrine at all. Zen is simply an invitation to experience God where he lives, where he is in his presence, here and now. There is no doctrine whatsoever. We always stress that Zen is an experience. The *word Zen* comes from the Sanskrit *dhyāna*. When Zen came to China, the Chinese searched for a sound that was similar to *"dhyāna"* and came up with "Ch'an" (one reference says Ch'ana). The characters with which they expressed this word are, on the left, "God," and on the right, "simple," literally, "the simplicity of God." So the meaning of the word as portrayed in the characters means, "God the way things are" or "God-Simple."

Since experiencing "the way things are" is what Zen is, then all we have to do is just *be the way we are.* If we do this, then as the Rōshi says, the *fact* of Zen will come to us. We will know that the divine goodness, which permeates all things, is really ours. To know something intellectually and to know it experientially are different indeed. We can know intellectually the properties of electricity, but that's nothing like being hit with a live wire!

An experience of Martin Buber comes to mind. As a young boy he loved nature, and one evening after supper, he was in the barn patting the nape of his pet horse, and something happened to him. Later, trying to put it into words, he said that the life force that came from the horse was the same life force that ran through his hands, the same life that runs through the earth, the same life that runs through the whole universe, and that somehow that life infused him at the instant of patting the horse. So, "all things are permeated with Divine Nature" became for him not a doctrine but a concrete reality.

As a college student, a now famous Catholic theologian was an articulate atheist. One day, not being able to concentrate on a boring lecture, he glanced out of the window and saw new young leaves sprouting from a tree. Suddenly something came through him. He was later to explain that the life coming through those new leaves was the same life that penetrated the tree itself, and was the same life that vivified him as he sat in the classroom. It was the same life that enabled everything to exist. Having experienced this, he could no longer be an atheist.

At that instant he could no longer have any doubt about the existence of God.

Let us not be misled by those words, "the existence of God." God does not have some kind of ethereal existence. The words represent an experiential realization of simple facts: leaves are green; the horse's neck is rough and hairy; the wind blows; and so forth. These simple facts enable us to be permeated with this Divine Nature and Presence.

The following lines of the *Song of Zen* are an explanation of how all beings are Buddhas. *As in the case of water and ice, there is no ice without water.* We would not say this if we depended only on our senses. When we feel water we know it is not ice, because ice does not feel like that. Ice is hard, our senses tell us. Our senses tend to delude us and say, "Ice does not feel like water, therefore, it is different and separate." But the *Song* says, "As in the case of water and ice, there is no ice without water."

Many times in our daily lives we are deluded by our senses so that we think things are different from what they really are. For instance, the Japanese are very good at massage. A good masseur can tell you whether you are tense or not, often sensing tension you yourself are not aware of. We tense up because we are not fully at home with ourselves and the way we are. The philosopher Heidegger says, "Let beings be." Let yourself be you as you are; the wonder of "you as you are" can never be expressed in words.

> *Not realizing that Truth is so close,*
> *Beings seek it far way—alas!*
> *It is like one who, while being in the midst of water,*
> *Cries out for thirst.*
> *It is like the son of a rich man*
> *Who gets lost in a poor village.*

In another translation we read, "Not knowing how close the truth is to them, beings seek it afar . . . what a pity!" Not knowing we are children of God, we are deluded into thinking we are miserable and distorted and separate. We feel separated because we are ignorant of the true fact of God. What is the root of this separation from our basic goodness? It is our preoccupation with ourselves and our attachments and desires. We tend to confront things and view them from our standpoint — I'm here, you're there — and we think that is the way things are! How sad that people think that! How sad that people go to the ends of the earth to seek for the truth that is right here!

The Kingdom of God is at hand. Open your hearts and welcome the good news. This basic message of Christianity cuts away the original sin that separates us from God. Before the creation of the world, we are made in the image and likeness of God. We are indeed the rich man's child, though we are unaware of our riches.

There is a parable in the Buddhist scriptures about the son of a rich man wanting to leave home and go to all the villages he had never seen before. Before giving permission, the father sewed a precious jewel in the collar of his son's robe. Everywhere he went, the son had with him inestimable wealth in that jewel secretly hidden in his collar, but of course he didn't know this. Eventually he ran out of money during his travels. He was hungry and dirty and tired, but unable to do anything about it, or so he thought. He knew nothing of the wealth he was carrying around! Each one of us possesses that richness, if only we knew where to look. And that is the exhortation of the opening of the *Song of Zen*, "Look, you have wealth with you . . . discover it . . . and put it to good use. Live it!"

The next lines are:

The reason why beings transmigrate through the six realms
Is because they are lost in the darkness of ignorance.
Wandering about from darkness to darkness
How can they be freed from the circle of birth and death?

Indian philosophy mentions six realms of living beings who keep on being reborn and dying without ever reaching eternal happiness, a kind of hellish existence of not being freed from suffering. These lines tell us that ignorance is the cause of suffering, which prevents us from seeing what we truly are. They are a comment on sin and ignorance and selfishness.

We wander from dark path to dark path. Our daily lives are filled with such things as melancholy and discouragement, greed and desires. This is true not only of human beings but of nations and all of human society . . . everyone is out for himself or herself. We are all in conflict with one another. I have an interest in a piece of land, so does someone else, and for both of us, only that one piece of land is adequate, so we are at odds. Governments are in the same situation, and this creates the kind of society where the powerful exploit the weak. Those who are exploited go on to exploit others, and the vicious circle continues. This is what is meant by transmigration, wherein we are unable to realize true happiness whereby we see things as they really are.

How are we freed from this birth and death cycle? Basically by the realization of what we are, or in other words, by awakening to the reality of ourselves, our True Selves. How do we awaken to this True Self? This happens when we see that we are permeated with the Divine Presence, as in the basic Zen saying: *"kenshō jōbutsu"* that is, to see into one's nature is by that very fact to become Buddha . . . to see and to accept that we are children of God, heirs of the universe, heirs of heaven!

The impediment to the freedom from birth and death is our own selfish orientation, where we turn into ourselves and see everything in terms of our own subject-object interests. Yamada Rōshi is always telling us to oust that subject-object dichotomy and let things be as they are. This is how we are able to see into our own nature. This is the core of our Zen practice.

Earlier we mentioned that our direction is toward wholeness. But we must try first of all to unify ourselves, to draw away from our disparate interests in this and that. Actually this "dispersion" is based on a selfish orientation, because it's always "I want this" . . . "I want that" . . . always a reference to "I." Thus we are dissipated in many things. If we are able to affirm things as they are, then there is no separateness at all.

As to the Zen of the Great Vehicle
No amount of praise can exhaust its treasures.
The six Ways to perfection, beginning with Giving,
Living a right life, and other good deeds,
Intoning the name of Buddha, Repentance, and so on,
All these come down to the merit of Zen sitting.

The usual translation of the first sentence is, "O, the *Zenjō* of the *Mahāyāna*," an exclamation of the highest praise, extolling the many virtues which arise from the *Zenjō*, which is the translation of the Sanskirt *samādhi*, "deep meditation." Samādhi or deep meditation is "to be unmoving" or "to be unmoved" in everything. It is unmoved, and yet it is the power that moves everything. In philosophic terms, it is the unmoved mover. In a similar vein, the basic subject of the *Kegon* or *Hua Yen Sūtra* is the life of the Buddha that shines through the universe. The dynamic mover of everything itself does not move. This is the way everything is in samādhi.

"O, the Zen of the Great Vehicle." The state of samādhi is itself unmoved, and yet is the power that moves everything. It is not just samādhi (or unmoved meditation) that we enter, but the very movement of the universe itself, into which we plunge ourselves as we enter this state. In our Zen practice we enter into that dynamism of the universe which is complete, perfect, fully calm, yet which itself is full of energy. In this calm originates the power which moves the whole universe. It is that into which we plunge ourselves as we participate in Zen.

The Zen of the Great Vehicle is in contrast with that of the Lesser Vehicle. The latter implies a selfish orientation, the kind of sitting that is a hindrance to true realization and a sidetracking from what Zen really is. Years of experience will tell us that to sit is to let oneself be as one is. Sitting this way, one eventually lets everything be as it is, and thus finds unity with everything. One may struggle with the tendency to sit mainly for oneself. Actually, one sits together with all beings in order to realize oneness and fullness. This is the essence of the Great Vehicle, or *Mahāyāna*.

To this be the highest praise, to the samādhi of the Great Vehicle, the dynamism that permeates the whole universe though in itself it is calm and still. This is the inner disposition we are called upon to achieve in our daily lives. We must be calm and yet dynamic. We are not agitated in our dealings with others. We neither push ourselves nor do we push others. We are to be what we are, and accept one another as we are. In so doing, the power that lies latent will naturally activate itself.

This is the object of praise. It is a state that encompasses all the other devotional practices. All are contained in Zen sitting.

SONG OF ZEN, PART III

Every thing, every moment is new! "Behold, I come to make all things new," says the Lord. So the newness of every moment is what we are called to taste and grasp. That is why the next line says, "The merit of even a single sitting in Zen erases the countless sins of the past," or as another translation has it, "One sitting sweeps away all ancient vices." In the eternal moment there is no past or future. It is simply the eternal now. We are living in the eternal present, before the foundation of the world and at the culmination of time, when all things in heaven and earth will be gathered as *One*, in Jesus Christ, as we read in Ephesians. We are called to taste and grasp that *now* at every moment of our lives. If we think of this with our intellect, it will lead to contradictions. So we must throw away thoughts to get to that infinite world, the world of the Essential Nature.

Where then are the evil ways that can mislead us?
The Pure Land cannot be far away..

This is a repetition of what has been said so far. It recalls for us the so-called realized eschatology we find in the gospel, especially in St. John, which gives us a resounding emphasis on the *Now*. An example is when Jesus went to the synagogue and read an ancient passage from the text of Isaiah and proclaimed clearly, "Behold, these words of scripture are fulfilled *now* before your very eyes." The Pure Land, therefore, cannot be far away; the Kingdom of God is at hand. Let us try to hear it. Listen to the word of God, the sound of God.

Those who even once, with a humble disposition
Are able to hear this Truth
Praise it and faithfully adhere to it
Will be endowed with innumerable merits.

Or as another translation puts it, "The one who hears the script but once, listens to it with a grateful heart, exalting it and revering it, gains blessings without end." Just once is enough! The one experience of Shakyamuni under the bodhi tree revolutionized his entire life. For many of us, it is the one true moment when we can really hear the Word and are enabled to see our True Selves. This moment will remain forever, and we will be changed forever because of that one experience.

There is a Chinese proverb every Japanese child memorizes when he or she studies Confucian thought. An approximate translation is, "When one is able to hear the Tao in the morning, one can die in peace in the evening." If one is really able to see the Truth, then that's enough . . . one is ready to die. Those were the words of Yamada Rōshi himself, immediately following his experience. It was so profound that it revolutionized his entire universe, and he was able to say, "I am ready to die." Even if I die at this moment, my life would have infinite value because of this one experience.

Those of us who have had small drops of Truth in that experience may be able to say the same. That drop at that moment is enough to make us realize our lives are of infinite value. Even if we die at that very moment, we have no fear of pain or death. We are ready for anything, because we have received an infinity of richness. There is nothing to lose. The Truth we experienced is obviously not a kind of exalted universal truth that one understands after laborious reasoning. It is the result of some little stimulus, the ticking of a clock, the clapping of hands, the breaking of a bucket—simple facts of daily existence, under our very noses! As the *Song* says, it is a tragedy if we go afar, looking for the Kingdom of God, for it is right here! We can't hear the things that are close and near to us! Let us listen to these truths, the simple facts of our daily living. The Word of God is speaking here. Our lives are called to fruition not in some glorious future, but with every fact in our daily existence. God is with us . . . the precise meaning of Christianity . . . God becoming human. When we grasp what it means to be human, then something will speak . . . the Word of God.

> *But if you turn your gaze within*
> *And attest to the Truth of essential-nature*
> *That Self-Nature that is no-nature*
> *You will have gone beyond mere sophistry.*

If you turn within and prove your own self-nature, you have gone beyond mere cleverness. It is not easy to "turn your eyes within yourself" because in the Essential World there is no within or without. On the practical level this is telling us that we are distracted by things outside ourselves, because we (as subjects) pursue them as objects, which automatically puts them "outside" ourselves. We listen to sounds "out there." We see things "out there." We relate to people "over there." The *Song* tells us to stop looking out and to look within. We do this by cutting out the distinction of outside and inside. Everything is seen from within, because we are all in the same world, inside the Kingdom, as we realize in Zen.

This, of course, does not mean that we look at our psychological impressions and reactions or both because that, too, is taking those impressions and reactions as objects, and puts us "outside" again! If this is a way of seeing that cuts through the subject-object distinction, how can the eye see itself? We will come to that in the next stanza of the *Song*.

"Attesting to the truth" means "to realize clearly." And in realizing our self-nature we find that in the actualization, it is no-nature. Now we have a contradiction. How is that? We have to go back to the fraction that Yamada Rōshi uses, with zero-infinity as the denominator. There is nothing there! We are nothing before the infinity of God. This is the scholastic doctrine, *creatio ex nihilo*, that says we are created out of nothing. Turning inward, we are called to reduce ourselves to that nothingness from which we were created, and we will see there the face of God.

The face of God is the face in whose image we were created. That's the face in the *kōan*, "Show me your original face before your parents were born." How can that be? We can't say "I was a twinkle in my father's eye," because he was not yet born. That face is the nothingness of our nature, before the foundation of the world, when we were created blameless and full of grace in the Lord. Show me that face of nothingness that participates in God's infinity! That cannot be accomplished through mere cleverness, because in analysis, it is a contradiction. From the standpoint of logic it is nonsense, so there is no use trying to define it. We are not talking about doctrine. This is a call to experience.

The gate of oneness of cause and effect is thrown open.
The path of the non-duality, non-threefoldness right ahead . . .

The relationship of cause and effect is something that is always mentioned in Buddhist philosophy, whenever we are sidetracked into intellectualizing. The second *kōan* in the *Mumonkan* talks about whether the enlightened man is free from cause and effect. The gist of this can be gleaned from this stanza of the *Song*: "Cause and effect are one . . . not two, not three, the path runs straight." If the path runs straight, what about the *kōan*, "Walk straight on a narrow mountain road that has 99 curves"? To break that *kōan*, you have to walk that straight path, no second, no third, just one. Zen always emphasizes the one, the single . . . not the abstract one, but each one concrete fact.

Form being the form of no-form
Going and coming back is right where you are.
Thought is the thought of no-thought.
Singing and dancing are the voice of Truth.

The "form and no-form, thought and no-thought," go together, from a Chinese phrase pronounced in Japanese *munenmusō*, "no thought, no image," the ideal of the Japanese monks. Actually, this is a bit misleading in words, because how can you have no thought, no-form when you are sitting and saying, "I have no thought"? That's already one thought! To say we have no thought or no form boggles the mind and pushes us into a corner. But we can't cut the vicious circle.

How can we have this no-form and no-thought? Simply by settling down and letting ourselves *be*. When we're hot, we just wipe off the sweat without reflecting on the heat. When we're thirsty and take a drink we are just one with the moment, being ourselves with the moment, fully, totally. Not to think, but to *be*, is the secret.

The second phrase, "Your going and coming back is right where you are" or, as another translation has it, "Your going and coming, never astray," means there is no coming or going, and yet, by always moving to and fro, one is always still. Nonsense again! We see our world moving in the phrase of Heraclitus, "Everything moves, everything flows." And yet another Greek thinker, Parmenides, says, "Nothing moves, everything is one." What we are seeking is a reconciliation of those two: everything moves, yet everything is still. Perennially moving, we are always still, which means we are where we are. We keep on moving dynamically and yet nothing moves, nothing has to move, everything complete and at peace. In the Kingdom of God there is no longer any sorrow or tears.

The last phrase in the stanza is "Singing and dancing are the voice of Truth." Singing and dancing are a full expression of the truth of the Dharma. Whatever we do, eating or drinking, we do in the Lord (I Cor. 10:31).

Another practical explanation is that when we dance, we do "*munen-musō*," no-form, no-thought . . . just dancing. I remember after the *sesshin* in Leyte that the Rōshi was watching us enjoy a dance party. As we lost ourselves in the merriment, he asked us very seriously, "How can you not attain *kenshō* when you know how to do this so well?" Whatever we do, let us be fully there, in that moment.

How boundless and free is the sky of samādhi,
How refreshingly bright, the moon of the Fourfold
    Wisdom!

We come to samādhi, the inner world of stillness, which manifests itself dynamically in the movement of the universe: "The clear blue sky with no trace of cloud to mar the gazing eye." Our eyes are delusions of ourselves, or our neighbors, or the phenomenal world. If we are able to break through those delusions, then everything becomes like a clear blue sky, and the moon is able to shine brightly. We don't even need a finger to point to the moon. All we have to do is let it shine in all its splendid brilliance.

At this moment, what is it you seek?
Nirvāṇa is right here before you
Pure Land is right here.
This body, the Body of the Buddha.

These last four lines are a summary. A more familiar translation is, "And what more indeed can we seek; here is Nirvāṇa itself revealed; this very place is the Lotus Land; this very body, the Buddha." Consider a circle. A circle! Everything is here, complete and total. What more indeed can we seek? The circle is perfect, but it is also zero, nothing! We are nothing, created out of nothing, and yet complete in our nothingness. That nothingness is precisely the key to our completion, perfection, peace and freedom, and its symbol is the circle.

"Here is Nirvāṇa itself revealed." Not way up in the so-called heavens, but right here under our noses. This basic doctrine has been sadly overlooked, and that is why Marx criticizes religion as being a pie in the sky. People look up to the sky for their fulfillment, which makes them neglect the here and now. Open your eyes, and open your hearts, the Kingdom of God is at hand.

"This very place is the Lotus Land." Let us not misunderstand this phrase to mean that we are already in heaven. There is still a whole world to be transformed! The whole of creation is groaning towards its fulfillment (Rom. 8:19). And yet with each act of groaning, the "already here" and the "not yet" come together. The Kingdom is realized and yet is still to be fulfilled. The contradiction becomes one in the Essential World. The here and now being fully whole and yet calling for a greater wholeness . . . God always exceeding himself . . . *Deus semper maior.*

The last phrase, "This very body, the Buddha," is not our image of the Buddha. "This very body" is a manifestation of what we Christians call the Son of God. Let us muse over what happens at Mass. The words of consecration are "This is my body." If we take away subject and object dichotomy here, what do we have? Just listen! This is my body. Who is "my"? If we think it is this 5'6" body, we are conscious of only a very small area of ourselves. We know from our dream images that we "drop" to a deeper level during sleep. We can go deeper than that again, far deeper than we can imagine, and that is where our True Self lives. Zen is simply an attempt to get down to that level, for only at that level can we say, "this body."

If we are only at the top level of our conscious selves, we are but little separate heads, and I am here and Jack is over there. We are different. But if we are able to go to a deeper level, we see the point where there is no division. We share "this body." Here we can resolve all contradictions and say all is one, or that A is equal to 3 or that 1 is 2, because at this point everything has *zero* for its denominator. At this level, we can say "this body," which manifests the Divine, not as a particular doctrine, but as a Christian proclamation that we are partakers, children of one Father. Who is this Father? Shapeless . . . formless . . . and we can't conjure an image in the imagination, for he is not a bearded old man! At this deep level, where there is no within or without, everything blossoms forth. From there we can "see" that we are all one. We are all to share in one another's lives, and thus from here compassion is generated.

What is compassion? Compassion is when we see suffering, and that suffering is our very own, not something apart from us. When we say, "To be one with the poor," means that we are able to see the suffering of the poor as our very own suffering. It becomes a kind of unavoidable imperative. Our very nature calls us toward that.

Yamada Rōshi is a very clear example of a man of deep compassion. If you read his articles, you will notice he always has references to world problems, to the problems of contemporary humanity. His heart is one with what he sees, precisely because he is truly living in the world where he no longer sees any separation between subject and object, himself and others. One is simply able to identify one's True Self in everything. This is the source of Buddhist compassion.

This is not only Buddhist compassion, but also Christian *agape* — to love one's neighbor as one's own self, on realization that there is no distinction between self and no-self.

When we can see from that perspective, Christian *agape* will really "speak." *Agape* is a sharing in that life, a sharing in the oneness of life in which we have been involved from the very beginning. We simply open ourselves to that. The compassion that enables us to be one with the suffering of others should be a natural outflow of our Zen. And it should flow out, not only to the suffering of others, but to all of creation with whom we were created in Oneness. It is in the cutting away of all differences, social and otherwise, that we are able to embrace one another.

6

The Heart of the Samaritan

People suffer. Things are happening everywhere. We are in a state of anguish and pain. If we look at the trends all over the world, we are faced with crisis and conflict and people hurting one another ... people immersed in violence and dying.

When we reflect on ourselves doing Zen, we see that we are "sitting," if not in a haven of peace and comfort, at least away from the chaos of the world. Let us not forget that we do so in order to enable ourselves to be more sensitive and to gain strength to bear that pain, and to open ourselves to its reality.

The following passage of scripture is presented with the caution that we are not going to do an intellectual exercise or make a commentary on scripture. We can easily be misled into doing that. I say misled, because in actuality we are faced with a *living thing*, we are presented with *food*, and that has nothing to do with analyzing. When presented with food, we are called upon to partake of it, to eat it! So it is with this attitude that we should enter into the scripture passage. Scripture reading should be bodily reading. We should read not only with our hearts and heads, but also with our whole being, getting into that living word and allowing that life to "be-come" with every pulse and with every breath.

On one occasion a lawyer came forward to put this test question to him: "Master, what must I do to inherit eternal life?" Jesus said, "What is written in the law? What is your reading of it?" He replied, "Love the Lord your God with all your heart, with all your soul, with all your strength, and with all your mind; and your neighbor as yourself." "That is the right answer," said Jesus; "do that and you will live." But he wanted to vindicate himself, so he said to Jesus, "And who is my neighbor?" Jesus replied, "A man was on his way from Jerusalem down to Jericho when he fell in with robbers, who stripped him, beat him, and went off, leaving him half dead. It so happened that a priest was going down by the road; but when he saw him, he went past on the other side. So too, a Levite came to the place, and when he saw him went past to the other side. But a Samaritan who was making the journey came upon him and when he saw him was moved to pity. He went up and bandaged his wounds, bathing them with oil and wine. Then he lifted him on to his own beast, brought him to an inn, and looked after him there. Next day, he produced two silver pieces and gave them to the innkeeper, and said 'Look after him; and if you spend any more, I will repay you on my way back.' Which of these three do you think was neighbor to the man who fell into the hands of the robbers?" He answered, "The one who showed him kindness." Jesus said, "Go and do as he did" (Lk. 10:25-37).

We tend to misunderstand the passage and see it as moral injunction to help our neighbor in need. Well and good, but this doesn't go far enough. It doesn't do full justice to what is being presented to us. It begins with the question of the lawyer, "What must I do to attain eternal life?" Whether we are aware of it or not, this is the very question we ourselves are asking in our hearts, although we may put it in different ways.

What is true living? What is genuine life? What is the life of the eternal now? What is eternal life whereby we are at one with our True Self . . . at one with the Universe . . . at one with every particular being . . . *the* genuine life?

And we don't have to refer to it as the life after we die, the life that we will go on living after death, for ages and ages. It is something that is before us here and now. It is the same reality that is indicated in another scripture passage, "The Kingdom of God is at hand." The *now* before us! How are we to partake of eternal life here and now?

It is not a matter of merit "because" we have done good for our neighbor. It is an interpretation of long standing that if we do a good deed, we gain merit, and go to heaven. That is a very limited interpretation of the text. It is much broader and deeper than that. It is something offered to us here and now.

What we are looking for in reading scripture is not the "meaning" of the text, but rather the key to the search we are all engaged in, the answer to the question, Who am I? "Who is my True Self?" *That* is the question we ask as we begin reading the scripture passage. Now, with that disposition, we are prepared to enter the text bodily, and not just intellectually, emotionally, or both.

We are hunting for eternal life! Well, that's what we're looking for in the *kōan Mu*. Now when we do this *kōan*, we breathe in and out with *Mu*, sit with *Mu*, and when we find *Mu* we will find eternal life, that True Self we are seeking.

It is not any different from the passage we just read from the Bible, which begins with the sentence, "You should love the Lord God with all your heart, with all your soul, and with all your strength, and with all your mind." These words are so familiar to us that they tend to go in one ear and out the other. But this time, let us ask ourselves, does this loving God with our whole mind involve some special kind of activity? Perhaps we can ask the same question in a different way: How do you love God with your whole mind while you're driving a car? . . . or when you're sleeping or when you're in terrible pain? Or how do you love God when you are sitting? How do you love God in every moment, and with every activity in daily life? This is not an additional thing we do, over and above all the little things we do from day to day. What is our day made up of? We get up, wash our faces, take breakfast, go to work, meet people, and so on. We do all those things with our whole soul, our whole strength, our whole mind. Then, how do we love God? What is eternal life in all the particular events of our daily life?

Now let us look at the second clause. This is no different, it is replete with the same fullness of content when we treat our neighbors as ourselves, with our soul, our whole mind, our whole heart, our whole strength. This aspect presents us with a more complete focus. This is well-illustrated in the story of the Good Samaritan.

Here I want to repeat that because we tend to take the drama as a moral injunction to help those in need, we easily misunderstand the text. It catches us in the old duality: us and those in need. We help someone, and then we feel good about it . . . self-satisfaction.

That's not quite what the passage gives to us. When we examine it, we find the word *compassion*. The original Greek word is *splanchnizōmai*, and means, literally, "to be moved in one's bowels." When this word is used, it signifies, "being moved to the very depths of one's being." Hence, the translation of *compassion* is "to suffer with." The pain of the person lying there on the road, as we read in the text, becomes the very pain of the one who finds the sufferer. It is no longer a case of being up on one's donkey saying, "Ah, too bad! That poor fellow!" from the outside. No! The Samaritan had compassion. At that very instant he saw through the barrier of self and the other, and the pain of the wounded man became his own. So he jumped off the donkey, treated the wounds, and made provision for shelter and care.

It is very important for us to see that the Samaritan did not act as a volunteer, nor did he perform a good deed for another, a meritorious act that would gain merit. He merely did instantly what he would have done for his own pain. This is what happens when one transcends duality, when one sees "the other" as one's own self.

Here I am tempted by one of the occupational hazards of being a philosophy teacher, to wander, to side-track, to go into more of the by-ways of defining compassion. But I will forego the temptation and limit myself to one digression. The *key* to entering this world of compassion is what we aim at in Zen when we say we try to cut through the barrier of duality, such as subject and object. In this particular scripture passage, the key is the pain. It is no longer "I" looking at "somebody in pain," but that very pain is mine! Instantly! My very own!

What we have to do to gain eternal life is given to us in this very significant story. What we must take note of is that all he did was simply the natural spontaneous result of breaking through the original duality of "I" and "the other." The Samaritan and the wounded man became *one* in pain.

Now in the last part of the story, Jesus asked, "And who do you think was neighbor to that man in pain?" The lawyer's answer was, "The one who had mercy." Christ responded, "Go and do likewise." Christ did not mean go and do what the Samaritan did. He threw his words out as a kind of *kōan* . . . do likewise . . . live that life of non-duality in which the pain of the person next to you is your own pain. We cannot live the life of non-duality in the abstract "pain of humankind." That doesn't exist. We can only live it in the pain of the actual person who has pain, like the person next to us.

Who are the persons next to us? They are, among others, those suffering the pain of illness and malnutrition, those deprived of the bare necessities of life, those driven from their homes by the greedy rich, those poor farmers, laborers and prisoners harassed by the military. It is essential that we do not see these people as "outside of ourselves." Their pain should be our very own pain. When we are able to transcend the duality, whatever we are called upon to do in the light of the present situation will flow from us naturally, spontaneously and instantly.

Our way is something fundamental, underlying all programs for action and social change: It is a way called com-passion . . . suffering-with. It is found right in Christian scriptures such as the passage we have been looking at.

The world of Zen is not at all different. The so-called enlightened person is characterized by the state of wisdom of nonduality, which flows naturally into compassion. Wisdom and Compassion are not two; compassion *has* to be based on nonduality, the condition of being *One*. Oneness is not something that breeds self-complacency, so that you can fold your arms and say, "I'm at one with the rest of the universe; let's have a glass of beer." (Nothing against beer, of course!)

The undercurrent is that the pain of one's neighbor is one's own pain. Given one's own particular individuality, the response will flow naturally. In that sense no one can tell us what to do.

We live in the way we must, in our response to the pain of our neighbor.

I was asked why some "radical" nuns have turned to Zen. Looking at the word *radical* in its true meaning we find it is telling us to return to the roots of our very being. Our roots are our nothingness before God's infinite nothingness.

I see our Blessed Mother as the epitomé of the radical, the enlightened person, the wisdom of non-duality. In the flowing compassion of the wisdom of her nothingness, in the total emptying of herself, the grace of God so enveloped her that there was no duality at all in her being. Her every action and indeed her whole life was a manifestation of the grace of God. That grace of God expressed its fullness in her life when it reached its culmination in her sharing the suffering of the Lord on the cross. And let us remember that that sharing was not just a matter of devotion or emotional attachment but the factual reality that his pain was her pain. She accepted his suffering for all humankind with her own body, her own compassion. Neither can we forget that we are also called to this. Therefore, in no way are we called to isolate ourselves from the rest of the world.

To the extent that we have found our True Selves, we can live true compassion. So there are steps and stages when we have to struggle and find our True Selves. Sharing suffering is not only one of the means, but it is also a place where we can *find* our True Selves. It is in the very persons of our suffering brothers and sisters, when that suffering becomes our own, that we discover the life of non-duality and compassion, lived so eminently by our Blessed Mother.

Neither was the Samaritan dominated by duality. Remember, the Samaritans were looked down upon by the Jews, who thought they had priority in salvation. The Samaritans were considered second-class citizens and were the oppressed of the time. The Samaritan, therefore, knew what pain was. He knew what it was to be despised. He was very attuned to the pain of one who was poor. And so there was no barrier for him when he saw someone else in pain. The Oneness with that person in pain was very natural.

As we grow into our Zen, we grow into our own naturality. We bodily realize the meaning of non-duality, the *Oneness* of non-duality. Some of you may be familiar with Martin Buber's experience of non-duality with a tree, which he described in his book, *I and Thou*. There are many ways you can look at a tree. Buber tells us we can analyze it, or note its artistry or color and so on, but he says, there's another way, whereby the tree is there. That is all. Not I looking at the tree, but just the tree! That's it. No subject, no object, just the tree. It brings to mind the Zen *kōan*, "What is the essence of Zen?" and the answer, "The oak tree in the garden." That is an expression of non-duality. Of course it doesn't have to be a tree; it can be anything—a bird, the tick-tock of the clock, or, as in the case of the Samaritan, the pain of another. Our going out to that particular instant spontaneously is what breaks the power of the ego within us, and so we are enabled to be one with the particular, whatever it may be.

In our catechism, there is the question "What is the fullness of life we are called to live? What is the Kingdom of God?" The answer given is the same as the Lord's answer to the lawyer in the story of the Good Samaritan: "Love the Lord your God with all your heart and all your soul and all your strength and all your mind." We have found that this is possible in all our little daily activities, like riding a jeep. The second part of the answer, "and your neighbor as yourself," leads us to consider that each and every one of those suffering in poverty and oppression in the world today is our neighbor, as well as the person sitting beside us in the jeep.

In Zen terminology we would say forsaking the "I," forgetting the ego and going out and meeting *Reality—that* is Eternal Life.

My last word is the same as the first word. Take all these words out of your head . . . there might be cobwebs there! Come to the here and now! Let us *be* the pain in our legs or the ache in our back! Right here, now! This is where Eternal Life is!

7

The Four Vows
of the Bodhisattva

The Bodhisattva, or seeker-after-wisdom, is none other than each of us, in earnest search for our true self, our "original face." In the vows of the Bodhisattva we make a great resolve comprising four items, which we call the "Four Great Vows." We do this at the commencement of our practice, as well as all throughout our search.

1. Living beings are innumerable—I vow to save them all.
2. Delusive passions and attachments are inexhaustible—I vow to extinguish them all.
3. The aspects of the Truth (Dharma) are countless—I vow to learn and master them all.
4. The way of enlightenment is peerless—I vow to accomplish it.

With this great resolve, the seekers after wisdom profess that they desire enlightenment not only for their own narrow self-satisfaction or individual salvation, but that they seek wisdom together with all living beings. The Bodhisattva therefore seeks the salvation of all living beings—a great resolve indeed.

Some of us may ask ourselves, How can I presume to save others unless I myself am saved first? How can I enlighten others unless I am first enlightened myself? These are very central and apt questions.

However, this mode of questioning is marked by a misleading assumption concerning myself in relation to others, to all living beings. It is a misleading assumption of separation. It can only be overcome by the experience of enlightenment itself, whereby I fully realize that I am in all living beings, all living beings are in me. It is the experience of enlightenment that breaks the barrier between myself and others. One who is still at a stage prior to this experience can only take it on faith for the moment, namely, that all living beings are one, partaking of one life, one reality. But this act of faith is bound to be rewarded by the actual vision of what it promises, when that moment comes.

Let us now take the four vows in their particular meaning and expression.

1. LIVING BEINGS ARE INNUMERABLE—I VOW TO SAVE THEM ALL

The first vow calls to mind the infinite number of living beings that have existed since the beginning of time, as well as those who will exist until the end of time. Whether time has an end or beginning should not be our concern here—for this is only a mode of expression.

"Living beings" in Buddhist terminology imply "living beings in this world of suffering," or in short, "suffering living beings." With this implied sense we are called to perceive the actual situation of the world today, with all its disorder and conflict and suffering. And we do not just say "suffering living beings" and let it go at that.

We have to see the 850 million of the world's five billion people who are on the brink of starvation. We must see those deprived of even the basic food, clothing, and shelter necessary for normal human life. They struggle to survive under unjust conditions and inhuman treatment under oppressive structures, while trying to assert their inviolable dignity as human beings, in the face of so many structural and man-made obstacles. We must see the countless numbers of people involved or dragged into racial, interethnic, intrapartisan, internecine conflicts and violent struggles, and the numberless individuals and families driven from their homelands by repressive and unbearable conditions who are left to fend for themselves in hostile or indifferent societies that treat them as burdens on the economy. We must see those numberless people who suffer discriminatory treatment because of race, creed, origin, sex, or mental or physical disability. This long list does not even mention the inner mental and spiritual sufferings of every sort, from separation of loved ones, to all the modes of existential or psychological anguish.

The central characteristic of a living being, indeed, is this capacity to suffer. Not only the capacity, but the actuality of being in suffering. What does the seeker-after-wisdom vow, when he or she vows to save all living beings in their suffering? Does the seeker mean to eradicate suffering, to save beings *from* their suffering? If so, what a presumptuous attitude that would be. As if one could be a universal savior!

The hint of an answer is found in one of those *kōans* given after the initial breakthrough to *mu*. "Save a wandering spirit (ghost)," says the *kōan*. The point of the *kōan* is to be able to overcome the opposition between myself and the wandering spirit, in other words, to be one with that wandering spirit in its search for salvation. Those who have passed the *kōan* may have caught the point that the way to save the wandering spirit is the very same as the way to save all living beings in suffering. *One must become fully at-one with the wandering spirit.* This becoming-one *is* the very salvation that one is called upon to accomplish.

"Save a child dying of hunger!" If one knows how to save the wandering spirit, one also knows that the real salvation of the child dying of hunger does not consist merely in giving food. No, it is something else, something much more fundamental. I remember a book entitled *The Wounded Healer*. This title somehow comes across with this very same point.

In order to understand what this vow means, the seekers-after-wisdom are called, first, to break the barrier between themselves and the dying child, between themselves and all living beings. With this understanding, one is opened to an entirely new perspective in looking at this world of suffering.

2. DELUSIVE PASSIONS AND ATTACHMENTS ARE INEXHAUSTIBLE—I VOW TO EXTINGUISH THEM ALL

Delusive passions and attachments are a consequence of our blind ignorance (*mu-myō*), rooted in clinging to a delusive ego; this is the cause of the actual suffering of human beings. The delusive ego is the direct cause of the starvation of billions on our planet today, the unjust and inhuman structures where so many are hemmed in, the violent struggles between groups and factions that cause a virtual war situation in many places, the ongoing destruction of the environment (that threatens the very survival of our planet) perpetrated by those out for their own profit—all these and all the sufferings and anguish of individuals can be traced ultimately to the blind and destructive working of and attachment to the delusive *ego*, which pursues narrow self interest at the expense of others.

The strong lord it over the weak. Those with political, economic and military power wield these over so many of those who are powerless. Groups and individuals struggle for the control of such power. This is the human story told and retold.

Delusive passions and attachments are embedded deeply in each of us, and this is why they are said to be "inexhaustible." They are like weeds that keep popping up left and right, even before we are aware of them. To vow to extinguish these seems again like vowing the impossible.

But the hint toward understanding this vow is the realization of where the root of these delusive passions and attachments lies. To see this root in the blind workings of the ego, which separates and distinguishes *my* selfish interests from those of others, which puts *my* own welfare above and before that of others, is to see where to attack the problem. In short, uprooting this ego, the source of that delusive distinction between myself and others, the cause of my separation from others, is the key to the extinguishing of the inexhaustible.

The practice of *mu* is one concrete path toward this. It is not the only one, but is indeed something like a short cut. To realize *mu* is to break the chains of the delusive ego and to be opened to a new realm, a new freedom.

3. THE ASPECTS OF THE TRUTH (DHARMA) ARE COUNTLESS—I VOW TO LEARN AND MASTER THEM ALL

There are so many things to be learned and mastered in one's search for wisdom. The rudiments of sitting, the introductory elements are but the prelude toward a treasurehouse of inexhaustible learning. And each step in the process introduces the forthcoming one, and one is ever filled with wonder as one proceeds on within the labyrinth, circling on toward the center.

Those who have broken through the initial barrier of *mu*, will find *kōan* after *kōan* waiting in challenge, each one presenting a shining aspect of a multifaceted and multilayered crystal. *One* crystal all in all, but with an inexhaustible measure of gleaming facets to admire one by one.

If we look at even one facet and truly master it, making it our very own, we have the key to the mastery of the rest. For each facet reflects none other than our very own original face! And once the initial gate is opened, we proceed, going deeper and deeper in mastery, approaching it from an infinite number of angles, through concrete *kōan* practice.

Even for those who have finished the program of *kōans*, there is no stopping from further learning and mastery: this only means that they are now ready to go on their own toward new dimensions. A Japanese saying goes: "There constantly awaits something higher, something deeper" (*ue ni wa, ue ga aru—oku ni wa, oku ga aru*), a journey to the infinite, whereby each stop presents an infinity in itself.

4. THE WAY TO ENLIGHTENMENT IS PEERLESS— I VOW TO ACCOMPLISH IT

In a famous passage Zen Master Dōgen says, "To learn and master the way of enlightenment is to learn and master one's True Self; to learn and master one's True Self is to forget oneself; to forget oneself is to realize oneness with the whole universe."

The vow to accomplish the peerless way of enlightenment,

then, is simply the vow to realize one's very own True Self. We are not in search of something out there beyond our present reach. We are not on a journey toward some place far off. T. S. Eliot has this line in his *Four Quartets*:

We shall not cease from exploration
And the end of all our exploring
Will be to arrive where we started
And know the place for the first time.

It is right before us, *here, now*, but to get to *this* place we must indeed embark on an endless and perilous journey. It is endless, because there is no stopping. To arrive does not mean to cease from further proceeding, because there are always greater depths to be fathomed. It is perilous, because there are many obstacles and pitfalls in the process. The delusive ego lurks at every corner, waiting to catch us unaware.

But Zen Master Dōgen's hint is precious. To learn and master oneself is to forget oneself: a paradox! The practice of *mu* is a practice of this self-forgetfulness. Here one learns to abandon oneself in every breath, with *mu, mu,* and *only mu.* What else is there? An abandonment of oneself in the present moment, in the present endeavor. To forget oneself is simply to abandon oneself in this way.

In the beginning, the dark night of the soul is a toilsome, irksome, painful process, an excruciating experience. But at the end of the tunnel, it is crystal clear, snow country, gleaming at every instant, the whole universe embraced! This is not an abstract universe, but the very warp and woof of our daily life and toil. Every step, every word, every glance, every smile at each chance encounter . . . the letter to be written . . . the floor to be swept . . . the newspaper vendor . . . the children playing in the streets . . . the displaced slum dwellers . . . the farmers threatened with eviction . . . the laborers on strike . . . the demonstrating students . . . the political prisoners. Human, all too human. Familiar, all too familiar. But we know them, alas, for the first time!

8

Zen and the
New Consciousness

*Conversations with Yamada Rōshi
and Father Lassalle*

INTRODUCTORY NOTE

Yamada Kōun Rōshi (born in 1907) is Zen Master and Head of San-un Zendō, or the Zen Hall of the Three Clouds, located in Kamakura, Japan. Since the late nineteen-sixties, after Yamada Rōshi took over the leadership of the Zen group practicing in Kamakura from the late Zen Master Yasutani Hakuun, many Christians, including lay Catholics, priests, sisters, seminarians, as well as Protestant ministers and lay persons, began to practice Zen under his direction, in addition to (and together with) the many Buddhist disciples already under his care. Among these, some have already completed the basic Zen training program and are now directing others in Zen practice in the United States, Europe, and Asia. Many of his Zen talks and lectures have been published in Japanese, and English translations of some of these are forthcoming. Already published is his commentary on the famous *kōan* collection called *Mumon-kan* (*Wu-*

wei-kuan). (See Yamada Kōun, *The Gateless Gate*, Los Angeles, Center Publications, 1979.)

Fr. Hugo Enomiya-Lassalle, S.J. (born 1898) has been a Jesuit missionary to Japan since 1929. He started practicing Zen meditation "to learn more about Japanese culture," according to his own account, and has written many books about his experiences. After receiving training from several different Zen Masters, he came into contact with Yamada Kōun Rōshi in the early nineteen-seventies, and has been the latter's faithful disciple ever since. He has completed the basic *kōan* training under Yamada Rōshi, but continues to come for guidance whenever he is in Japan. (He spends a good part of each year in Europe directing Zen retreats in different Houses of Meditation.) It was his pioneering effort that enabled Christians to see the possibilities of deepening their spiritual life with the practice of Zen.

The author of the present volume is privileged to be able to learn from and dialogue with these two giants whose spiritual influence will be felt long after their time. The subtitle of this volume "Zen Spirituality and the Social Dimension" is also an underlying theme of the following conversations.

DIALOGUE OF LIFE

R. Habito: It was in the late sixties and early seventies that an increasing number of Christians, both religious and lay, began to gather around as Zen disciples of Yamada Kōun Rōshi in Kamakura. It was indeed a very rare phenomenon in those days, having a Zen *sesshin* under the direction of a genuine Buddhist Zen Master participated in by both Buddhists and Christians alike. At dawn, while the Buddhists chanted their *sūtras*, the Christians gathered in another room of the Zen Hall to celebrate the Eucharist. Other than this particular period, everything else was done together without distinction—a true sharing of life, on the part of both groups. I was still in my studies in the Jesuit theologate then, preparing for ordination to the priesthood, and Fr. Lassalle, being the only priest at that time, would be the celebrant at the Eucharist. And this practice continues with every Zen *sesshin* now held at the San-un Zendō, and as there are always several priests present, we take turns being main celebrant.

Such a "dialogue of life" has been made possible by the great vision of Yamada Rōshi, wherein now Buddhists and Christians transcend their sectarian boundaries and share in the same life of Zen. This is certainly evidence of a new consciousness arising that is grounded on their Zen experience.

May I ask the Rōshi, what particular points do you keep in mind as you direct Christians in the Zen practice?

Yamada Rōshi: You see, many Christians have been coming to me for guidance in Zen, and naturally one of the very first questions many of them ask me is whether they can remain as faithful Christians in coming to practice Zen. And I always answer them that they need not worry about forsaking or losing their Christianity. I tell them that Zen is not a religion and they do not have to think of it as such, in the sense of a system of beliefs and concepts and practices that demands exclusive allegiance. No, Zen is something other than that, and so I can tell Christians that they do not have to throw away their Christianity as they come to Zen. What Zen is, and how it is different from Christianity as I see it, I will not speak of right now.

R. Habito: Fr. Lassalle, what led you to start practicing Zen in the first place? I understand that you had already been in Japan for a good number of years and had played an important role in the building of the Japanese mission of the Society of Jesus even before the outbreak of the Second World War. It was in this context that you came to some Buddhist for instruction in Zen. What led you to this practice of doing Zen?

Fr. Lassalle: To answer in a roundabout way: Actually, when I was a young Jesuit doing my studies for the priesthood in Germany, I volunteered for the missions. I was impressed by the challenge in Africa, especially how people were living under very strict conditions of poverty, and how there were still slaves, and so forth, and I read a book entitled *From Cape Town to Zambesi* about some Jesuits who took a journey on an ox cart. I was in my second year of novitiate, and the German province was then entrusted with the Japanese mission when I wrote my letter volunteering for Africa. So I received an answer directly from Fr. General saying that it was not the will of God that I go to Africa, and thanking me for volunteering for Japan! So that is how I found myself being assigned to Japan.

R. Habito: What an interesting twist of providence!

Fr. Lassalle: So that is the story of my communication with Fr. General! And I said to myself that if I am to go to Japan, I must learn about the culture there. It was at that time that I started reading the books written by D. T. Suzuki and learned that Zen had a profound influence on Japanese culture, and was thus convinced that if I wanted to learn about the Japanese mentality I also must learn about Zen. When I came to Japan in 1929, I started to sit on my own, without any instruction. Then I started visiting some Zen monasteries, and received some directions. After that we had a group that practiced Zen sitting, after I was assigned to Hiroshima. In Tsuwano there was a Sōtō Zen monastery, where I did my first Zen *sesshin*. I was Superior of the Jesuit Missions at that time.

R. Habito: How did the other Jesuits react to your going to a Buddhist monastery to practice Zen?

Fr. Lassalle: I remember a priest who was worried about me, and warned me that if I continued such practices I might lose my faith! And there was a brother who kept murmuring, "What is this Father Lassalle up to now, going to the Buddhists and all?"

R. Habito: How would you describe the experience of your first *sesshin* at Tsuwano?

Fr. Lassalle: At that time I got such a deep impression that I wondered if we could not adapt these practices among Christians. So I gave a talk to some sisters and encouraged them in the ways of meditation that I learned from Zen. Then I organized a group of Christians to sit together in the Zen manner, and they were very happy, for they told me that they thought since they had become Christians they were not allowed to do such practices! So I was encouraged, and we continued sitting together regularly; we were even able to build a Zen Dōjō (hall) of our own in Kabe, near Hiroshima. Unfortunately the building had to be torn down after the war because the local government needed a place to build a pump for electricity, and they offered to find another place for me, but the Society did not want me to build another hall.

R. Habito: When did you start doing Zen with Harada Sogaku Rōshi?

Fr. Lassalle: That was after the war. There were many things destroyed by the war, and we were engaged in the process of rebuilding. So for a while I was busy as Jesuit superior in building the memorial cathedral in Hiroshima. But when that was finished I made a fresh start with Zen and inquired at Eiheiji, the central temple of the Sōtō Sect, and they recommended that I go to Harada Rōshi. The latter was quite surprised, because at that time he was not in good standing with the Eiheiji people. I was with him for about five or six years and received the *mu kōan* from Harada Rōshi. After he died I tried to continue with his successors in the temple, but did not get too far. So it was after a while that I went to Yamada Kōun Rōshi for direction, and that is where I am now. This was since the early 1970s.

CHRISTIANITY AND ZEN

Yamada Rōshi: There are some questions I would like to ask Christians who come to me for direction in Zen. I have been wanting to ask these questions for a long time now, but I have kept them to myself, as I felt these may just confuse Christians as they begin their Zen practice. But I feel confident I can ask these of both of you now. First, why did you not just continue doing meditational practices following your own Christian tradition instead of coming to Zen? Was there something lacking in Christianity that led you to seek something in Zen, or did you have some dissatisfaction with Christianity that led you to Zen? And also a question to Christians who have had the Zen experience through the *mu kōan*: How would you express this experience in your own Christian terms? And a third question: For those who have had the *mu* experience there is given the *kōan* about the origin (*kongen*) of *mu*. How would you answer a question about the origin of God?

Fr. Lassalle: For me it was not a question of something lacking in Christianity, but that I wanted to learn more about the Japanese mentality. I wanted to go deeper into the culture and spiritual treasure of the people I have been called to be with. That is why I began the practice of Zen. And as far as the continuance of practices of Christian tradition, it was actually my contact with Zen that enabled me to appreciate better the wealth that is found in Christian tradition, especially the mystical tradition in Europe, including the German and the Spanish mystics. I have written about this in my books about Christian spirituality in encounter with Zen mysticism.

R. Habito: For me it was an attempt to learn from another tradition that led me to Zen in the first place. I first joined a Rinzai Zen *sesshin* soon after coming to Japan, and it left such a deep impression on me that I naturally wanted to go on, and that was when I was introduced to your Zen group. Of course I began Zen with the motivation of delving deeper into the question Who am I? This I think puts us at the roots of the matter, the rock-bottom starting point for anyone starting Zen.

However, having already been through the experience of a two-year Jesuit novitiate, including the month-long spiritual exercises of St. Ignatius, I could say I was not starting from scratch. I had already gone though a somewhat rough period of self-searching and God-searching in my late teens, ever since my university days in the Philippines, and so all this was behind me when I started Zen. So for me the *mu*-experience had been prepared for by several stages of believing, doubting, understanding a little, doubting again, and so forth. When I look at the diary I was writing in those days I wonder at the various turns and crossroads I was passing through. But anyway, for me the *mu*-experience, triggered by my working on the *kōan* of Jōshu's dog, literally shook me inside out, and kept me laughing and even crying for about three days, as I remember. People around me must have thought I was going crazy then. I can only say at this point that the experience enabled me to see the truth, the forcefulness, the real reality of what Paul wanted to express in Galatians 2:20 — "It is now no longer I that live, but Christ in me!"

So to answer Yamada Rōshi's first and second question in the same breath, I came to Zen in the search for my True Self, and the *mu*-experience was its discovery, the discovery of my total nothingness. And yet this total nothingness is also total everythingness, the discovery of an exhilarating world of the fullness of grace surpassing all expectations, active even before

the beginning of the world (Eph. 1:1-11), and one can only exclaim again with Paul, Who can fathom "the breadth and length
and height and depth," and Who can "know the love of Christ
which surpasses all knowledge"? (Eph. 3:18-19).

And if you ask the origin of all this, I can only admit I don't
know. One can only humbly receive, from moment to moment,
the fullness of grace.

Yamada Rōshi: I see. I have always accepted Christians as
disciples with the implicit understanding that there is something
in common that can be shared, although I do not know much
about Christianity as such. However, it seems to me from what
I learn from those Christians I have come in contact with that
Christianity itself has changed over the years. Or maybe I have
had a sort of different idea of Christianity before, and it is that
idea that has changed.

R. Habito: Well, yes and no. Before the Second Vatican Council, held over twenty years ago, there were certain fixed notions
associated with Christianity giving the image of a rigid, closed,
and dogmatic set of beliefs developed by highly abstract theological speculations of medieval theologians, and linked with a
moralistic stance on the world often accompanied by a "holier
than thou" attitude toward other persons. Christians also gave
the impression that they had a monopoly on the Truth and even
had the notion that there was "no salvation outside the church,"
and interpreted this in quite a narrow way.

Fortunately, or should we say through the work of grace, the
Second Vatican Council encouraged a "return to the wellsprings" (*ad fontes*) of Christianity, and gave value to the attitude of going back to the experiential roots of the Christian
message as expressed in the scriptures. So now we are able to
take Christianity for what it was originally, that is, a message of
total liberation based on an encounter with the divine mystery
in and through the humanity of Jesus the Christ, Son of God.
So Christianity ultimately boils down to this basic religious experience of encounter, that is, of "divinity-in-humanity."

Yamada Rōshi: Recently one of my disciples, who is a Be-
nedictine nun, presented to me a book written by a German
Catholic priest, subtitled "Foundations for Buddhist-Christian
Dialogue." It was written by Hans Waldenfels, S.J., and the title

of the English translation is *Absolute Nothingness*. I was very much impressed with the contents of the book, and it led me to see that what you Christians call God may not be too different from what we are concerned with in Zen. Just the other day I had a meeting with four Catholic priests who have finished the Zen *kōan* training, and during our free discussion I asked them about this, and all of them seemed to agree on the common ground of what you call God and what we are concerned with in Zen. Fr. Lassalle came later, and he also shared the same view.

R. Habito: Yes, we are now dealing with something that cannot be adequately captured by words and concepts, and if we see things in this perspective, that is, the limitations of the words and concepts that we are using in our dialogue with each other, and are able to see beyond these limitations, then we are able to partake of that sense of communality, that we are breathing the same air and living in the same world.

It seems we have to overcome our one-sided ideas of God as a Super-Person, up there somehow like a Grandfather in the Sky, with a white beard and all, watching everything, and also understand that God is a Non-Person, the ground of all things. Here we are dealing with two concepts, "Person" and "Non-Person," but we have also to deny them both. We have to keep coming back to the experiential ground of our theological language.

ZEN AND SOCIAL CONCERNS

Yamada Rōshi: I understand that the pope as the head of the Roman Catholic Church is quite concerned with the salvation of humankind, and I admire him for this. But I can say that it is not just the efforts of the pope alone that can save humankind. We must all join hands in our common effort. Zen and Christianity can join hands, and we can be together in this common goal.

And to me, one of the major tasks facing humankind in this day and age is the problem of poverty, or rather the solution to the problem of the poverty of many people here on earth today. This cannot be accomplished by the United Nations alone, nor by the Vatican alone, evidently. This may be a task that will take us a hundred or two hundred years perhaps, although I have a friend who is an economics professor who says that it need not take that long.

R. Habito: Quite an optimist, he is! But this question brings us to the issue of the relation of Zen to our historical and social realities. How would you look at the nature of our involvement with the world? This is the very important question of the relation of Zen practice to social action.

Yamada Rōshi: Well for one thing, if people are hungry the first thing is to enable them to eat. For in such a situation they are in no position to listen to anything else, much less to talk about Zen or Christianity. One must first of all be able to partake of the minimum necessities of life to be able to proceed from there. But again, it is not good to live in luxury. I always stress what I call *"hin-gakudō,"* or learning the way with a poor and simple life. I have written about this in our Zen group's bimonthly magazine, the *Kyōshō*. Unfortunately, in recent times young people have become too used and attached to comfort and luxury. This was not the case when we were young.

R. Habito: Contemporary Japan seems to be intoxicated with its materialistic achievements, at the expense of basic human values.

Yamada Rōshi: I have high hopes for your country, the Philippines. In the next fifty or hundred years I am sure it will become a strong and great country. Not strong in the sense of being able to win a war, I hope. If only every individual can muster that innate strength given to help in the building of society! And that is where I think Zen can be a great source of strength also.

R. Habito: Through your guidance there are now several persons in the Philippines with your authorization to teach Zen there. Ten years ago, when Sr. Elaine MacInnes began sitting with a small group, those who came belonged to the middle-class sector and above. Recently there are more and more persons from the grassroots sectors, even from urban poor areas, who are learning to sit in Zen. I recall one sitting session I attended mainly for a group of about forty people from a poor district in Manila held at a retreat house run by Catholic sisters.

After the sitting session and the shared lunch, they all joined the rally of the farmers in front of the Presidential Palace in Malacanang, demanding land reform and basic changes in society. It was quite a natural outflow in that context.

Now I would like to ask Fr. Lassalle how he views this question of Zen practice and social involvement.

Fr. Lassalle: I see it in terms of the coming about of the new consciousness for humankind. This new consciousness transcends the traditional way of looking based on the subject-object polarity, that treats others as "objects" confronted by me as a "subject." This new consciousness goes beyond this opposition, and there comes with it an awareness of being one with all. It is this new consciousness that will become the basis of a person's social relations and way of involvement with society.

R. Habito: I would like to consider a little more what Fr. Lassalle here calls the emerging "new consciousness." There is the case of the individual who is only aware of his or her "subjective consciousness," and thus relates with others, with nature, and so on, in opposition. He or she only sees a very limited area of reality from this vantage point. This is like the visible part of the iceberg. But actually the True Self goes much, much deeper. First, there is the area of the subconscious, activated during sleep, as during dreams. Then there is a deeper area of what C. G. Jung called the collective unconscious, which is shared by human beings throughout history, as evidenced in common patterns in myths, symbols, archetypes. But even this area does not yet touch what Yamada Rōshi would call the "essential world" in Zen. It is what we can call the "phenomenal self."

The breakthrough beyond the subjective consciousness, going deeper than even the subconscious and the collective unconscious, through that realm where opposites coincide, where there is no longer subject nor object, no this nor that, no yes nor no — the world of emptiness — is our *mu*-experience in Zen. This is where one awakens to the basic fact of being one with the whole universe, as well as with each and every particular thing at hand, like this flower, that mountain, the sun, the moon, the stars; it's none other than myself! This is what enabled the Buddha to exclaim, "Above the heavens, beneath the heavens, no other one to be revered but I!" (*Tenjō-tenge, yuiga-dokuson*).

If this statement is misunderstood, it can be read as the height of blasphemy and egocentricity, but understood properly, it is an exclamation of the world of emptiness that is also the world of oneness with every particular thing in this whole universe. There is no other than I, and there is no such I! A conceptual contradiction indeed, but there is no other way to express it.

And from this perspective, where everything becomes manifest "as it truly is" (*yathābhūtaṁ*) in Sanskrit, or *nyojitsu-chiken* in Japanese), everything is seen with the Eye of Wisdom. It is in the light of this Eye of Wisdom that true compassion arises, for all the pains, the joys, the sufferings, the cries of everyone in the universe are as such my own pain, my joy, my suffering, my cry. It is only from this perspective that genuine works of compassion can come forth. It is not at all like that shallow kind of "pity" for others where one looks at those in suffering as it were from a perspective outside of that suffering. Here in the world of emptiness one is plunged right into that suffering as one's very own.

So a straightforward look at our present world as it is will manifest the state of suffering of countless living beings, those suffering in the midst of dehumanizing poverty, where malnourished babies die every minute, and where many continue to die victims of violence both individual and structural. All this is *my very own* suffering, and my body is wracked with pain from all sides. And I cannot remain complacent and unconcerned; I am literally inspired by an inner dynamism to be involved in the alleviation of this pain and suffering, in whatever capacity I am able. I am reminded of the image of the goddess of mercy (*Avalokiteśvara* in Sanskrit, or *Kuan-Yin* in Chinese, *Kanzeon* in Japanese) with a thousand hands, reaching out all over the world to those who are suffering.

Now may I ask both Fr. Lassalle and Yamada Rōshi for your concluding comments, especially on the tasks of the Zen-Christian dialogue for the future?

Fr. Lassalle: I would like to quote Jean Gebser, who speaks from the perspective of what I have been calling the emergent new consciousness. He says that we cannot foresee in detail what will come about, but things will by themselves come in the right way. We cannot speak of it in detail because we are dealing with a dimension beyond concepts. One can of course imagine certain possibilities of this and that particular thing, but the most important thing to be said in this aspect is that the extreme contradictions are overcome, and this is the crucial point. Unfortunately many people are not yet in the position to accept this. Recently I received a letter from a person who heard one of my talks in Germany, who said, "We Christians do not need all that emptying business—we already have Christ!" It was a very polite letter, but unfortunately I think it missed the point, for "Christ" here can become an idol, a concept that we need to empty ourselves of precisely in order to meet the real One, in this world of emptiness.

Yamada Rōshi: As I have said before, I am of the impression that Christianity is not at all the way I used to think it was, with just a rigid system of beliefs and concepts. There seems to be something there in common with what we are concerned with in Zen. Now in the many tasks we face in the world today, not any one of us can do the task alone apart from the others. We must join hands in bringing about a world that is One.

R. Habito: Thank you very much. We are in a world situation that can be described well in terms of the Burning House Parable in the Lotus *Sūtra*. In short, our living place called this world is already about to crumble, not only with the nuclear threat, but with continual violence based on ideological and even religious conflicts, with the increasing gap between the rich and the poor, and with ecological disasters that are in great part human-caused. And yet we are still wallowing in our ignorance, concerned only with our petty selves and our little selfish games. With the realization of what Fr. Lassalle calls the new consciousness, or in other words, with the emptying of this petty self-centered "subjective consciousness" toward the manifestation of what Yamada Rōshi calls the Essential World, the world of emptiness and thus precisely the world of Oneness, perhaps a way out of this Burning House will make itself apparent.

9

Kuan-Yin with a Thousand Hands

Why do many Zen enthusiasts show lack of concern for problems of society, issues of justice, and so forth? Indeed, why *do* so many, and not only the so-called Zen enthusiasts, show lack of concern for problems of society and issues of justice?

It is precisely this lack of concern of so many, one could dare to say, that is *causing* those problems of society, those situations of exploitation and oppression and injustice. Indifference to such problems enables the forces of greed, ignorance and ego-attachment, individual as well as corporate, in their various forms, to hold their sway and wreak havoc on our earth, leading to our present extremely critical and destruction-bound situation. Countless victims lose their lives daily, many others continue to live exploited and dehumanized, while many just go on leading lives centered on their own narrow little selves or their narrow little circles of concern. And this little circle of concern can be just on the level of "my career" or "my success" or "my family and friends," or even on a higher level of "my salvation" or "my religious mission."

For as long as this "salvation" or even "religious mission" remains confined within the boundaries of the individual or collective ego, drawing a line between what is "mine" and what is "thine," then one maintains a divisive factor in one's life that contributes to the problem. If one turns to Zen mainly for "*my*

95

peace of mind" or "*my* enlightenment," then unless there is a radical overturning of this attitude somewhere along the way, one's practice of Zen itself becomes a mere glorified form of ego-centered activity, and therefore something divisive.

Recently I met an American contemplative (Christian) monk who told me that before he entered the monastery he was a student activist who gave his all to the peace movement during student protests in the sixties in the United States. Then he realized that he was going in circles and getting nowhere and burning himself out, and that is when he decided to enter the monastery to become a contemplative. He added that he feels he is now making his contribution to peace precisely in being a contemplative, in being faithful to the religious life and praying for peace and for justice.

I mentioned this to Brother David Steindl-Rast, who is himself a contemplative (Benedictine) monk residing in California, and who also is quite an active participant in peace movements and finds himself often in the forefront of human rights activities and anti-nuclear protests in his area. I asked for his view on the matter. Let me summarize briefly what came out of a long conversation with Brother David, who for me remains a source of inspiration.

It is true that one can participate in peace movements, human rights activities, and so on, perhaps with a great amount of social concern and interest in the well-being of others, but this participation can be mingled also with some kind of self-righteousness or even some veiled form of self-seeking. In such a case one constantly needs to be purified of these elements in order that actions and ways of relating with others not be destructive and divisive. A sensitive and sincere social activist realizes this need of purification, and can and ought to turn to contemplation and prayer in this context.

Further, the contemplative vocation belongs to a hallowed tradition not only in Christianity, but in Buddhism, and in practically all the other major religions as well, and the contribution of these holy men and women who have devoted their lives to prayer and contemplation cannot be measured in quantifiable terms.

However, Brother David warns, we can also become *attached*

to our prayer and contemplation, and thus possibly fail to open ourselves to what God demands in a particular situation. "Go away, don't bother me; I am in contemplation," we can say to God knocking at our door asking for a drink of water or for a signature on a petition. We can *institutionalize* our prayer and contemplation and let them become another attachment rather than something that liberates.

No, the fruits of genuine contemplation precisely enable one to be totally free of all ego-attachments, to become a more viable instrument of peace. This is especially so for Christians with religious vows, as they are freed from family concerns, from financial concerns, and are enabled to be a little bit more "agile" than others. Thus, Brother David continues, since he does not have to worry about a family or his job or his reputation, he is totally free to put himself in the forefront of a peace demonstration or at an anti-nuclear sit-in and not be afraid of being arrested. "I can pray and contemplate as well in jail as in a monastery cell, or better, even."

This meeting with two Christian contemplative monks reminds me of a parallel again of two monks, this time in the Theravāda Buddhist tradition. One of them I happened to meet in an international religious conference in the United States, and I joined a *vipāssana* meditation session he conducted. The meditation theme was on generating *Mettā* or friendliness toward all living beings, and as he launched us off to a good start in paying attention to our breathing, he went on to suggest evoking a feeling of friendliness first toward one's body, part by part, from the foot to the head, and then toward other persons that came to mind, and then toward a wider and wider field, to include all living beings in the whole world, desiring their happiness and well-being.

The first part of the meditation went off rather well, and then our director-monk continued by suggesting that we concentrate on some pain we may have, say a pain in the leg or in the back: just to *be aware* of that pain, without attaching any value judgments or desires such as "I want that pain to disappear." After a while we will be able to accept the pain *as* pain, and live with it, and no longer consider it to be *suffering*, he explained. In other words, if one does not associate such ideas as "pain is undesirable" or "I want relief," which are actually judgments already based on ego-attachment, with the bare and "neutral" fact of the pain itself, then pain ceases to be suffering, but just mere pain, which one is now able to accept and live with, instead of making one miserable in the desire to eliminate it.

The Theravāda monk then gave us a concrete example of how meditation can calm us down, give us peace of mind and friendly and compassionate feelings toward all living beings in the universe, in this *vipāssana* session that he directed.

However, after the session I was overcome by a nagging doubt, and I regret not having had the opportunity to question the monk about it afterward. The question that lingered on in my mind was this: If this kind of meditation produces that kind of effect of calming us down, making us able to accept things as they are without injecting our ego-centered desires, well and good. But does it not also make us numb to the *real* suffering of others, the poor, the hungry, the exploited, the victims of structural and actual violence in this world of ours? Are we just dismissing them by simply having "friendly feelings" and "wishes for the well-being" of actual sufferers, from a conjured euphoric state of "contemplativeness"? In other words, does not this kind of practice tend to extinguish that passion for justice, that rightful indignation at the suffering of fellow-living beings, and thus become like cold water thrown unto the fire whereby Jesus wanted to set the whole world aflame?

To confirm my suspicions, the monk who directed this meditation session, though admired and looked up to by many for his unquestionable self-discipline and for his kindness and gentleness in dealing with those around him, was criticized at another religious meeting for lack of interest and sensitivity to certain socially-related issues that naturally should have concerned anyone living in his area.

But, fortunately, a second Theravāda monk I met in Thailand quelled my incipient disillusionment with *vipāssana* meditation practice.

I met this second monk as (again) I joined a *vipāssana* meditation session he was conducting for a group of student activists and social workers from Bangkok. Not yet quite forty, he related how he himself had been a student leader during the tumultuous years in Bangkok in the early seventies. He came to a point where he wanted to give himself totally to the people in the best way he could, and he was faced with a decision of whether to go to the hills to join the communist guerillas or to become a Buddhist monk. He chose the latter, became a disciple of the well-known monk Buddhadāsa Bhikku, who lives in the southern part of Thailand in semi-contemplation and welcomes anyone who would care to come for *vipāssana* meditation with him. Now after many years of *vipāssana* practice himself, he is able to direct others in meditation and has written several books in the Thai language on questions of meditation and social involvement.

"My hope is to be able to get my activist friends in the slums of Bangkok and in the countryside to do *vipāssana* on the one hand, and to get my fellow monks to go out to the slums and to the farms to meet the people there and know their situation, on the other." And so he is doing just that, directing *vipassāna* sessions especially for those involved in tasks of social change, getting monks out to the slums and to the impoverished farmside to meet people who are concerned and involved in those tasks of social action, so that there can be a stimulating exchange.

This second monk is himself quite active in providing support for a Buddhist-Christian center for development in Bangkok and, together with those working in this center, envisions a future for the Thai people that hopefully will enable them to ward off the destructive effects of Western consumerism by going back to their own cultural and religious roots, back to the basic values presented by Buddhism with regard to respect for life, respect for nature and so forth.

For this second monk, meditation practice, far from benumbing him to the real suffering and pain of others, heightens his awareness of these realities and provides the inner dynamism for him to continue in his manifold tasks in the reconstruction of society.

Reflecting on these encounters we are led to ask: What makes the difference between a meditative or contemplative practice that makes people turn within themselves in a contented and semi-euphoric state, and one that makes them more sensitive to the reality of pain and suffering in the world and to their place in that very pain and suffering, and thus spurs them to deeper involvement in the social dimension?

I cannot answer for the various types of meditation or contemplation, Christian or Buddhist, but will try to limit myself to what I know of Zen.

I have mentioned that there are three goals of Zen practice: 1) the development of the power of concentration, 2) the attainment of self-realization or enlightenment, and 3) the actualization or personalization of this enlightenment in one's everyday life, in every aspect and every dimension of one's total being. Now if one takes the first goal and centers one's Zen on the development of the power of concentration, one can indeed after a time notice the change in one's perception of things; as a natural result of sitting efforts and efforts at awareness, one is more able to have a sense of wholeness in one's life, to have a wholesome feeling in day-to-day existence, and to appreciate the little things that go on around one, even be more gentle and kind and friendly toward all beings that come one's way.

But without the arrival at the second goal, all these "natural results" of one's sitting efforts still leave one unsettled about the basic questions of existence, the basic questions of life and death. Who am I? What is my ultimate fate? How am I to relate to my neighbor? Such questions remain unanswered and are not solved by concentration alone.

It is the realization of one's True Self, that flash of seeing into one's original nature, that truly liberates one from that basic ego-centeredness, in realizing the empty nature of all things and the interconnectedness of all things in their emptiness. It is this realization that truly settles one's mind and heart, one's total being, that frees one from the fear of death, from the attachment to life, or vice versa. (I refer the reader here to the chapter on the *Heart Sūtra* on Liberating Wisdom for a treatment of various aspects of this enlightenment experience or realization, which is personal liberation.) And it is this same experience whereby I am able to see the true basis of my relationship to my neighbor, to society, to the whole world.

In Christian terminology this enlightenment experience is the realization of one's place in the whole Body of Christ: "This is My Body, which is to be given up for you" (Lk. 22:19). And thus,

"We, though many, are one body in Christ, and we are individually members of one-another" (Rom. 12:5). It is not just a "logical consequence" that I become involved in the suffering of others, but an *unavoidable inner exigency*; it is *my own* pain!

This oneness with all living beings in all their "joys and hopes, griefs and anxieties," especially with "those who are poor or in any way afflicted" (*Gaudium et Spes*, 1) is no longer just a pious platitude, but constitutes a central aspect of one's mode of being, permeating every aspect of one's daily life.

Thus the third goal of Zen consists in the process of letting this realization permeate one's total existence. As was mentioned before, *kōan* practice is geared toward this permeation, as each *kōan* deals with a concrete and particular facet of ex-

Kuan-Yin with a Thousands Hands

istence that brings one back to the roots of the experience of enlightenment. Through the *kōans* I am invited to *actually* experience my oneness in being with, say, a dog, a cat, a cow, or the stars in heaven. But let me stop here lest I reveal too much of what goes on in the interview room with the Zen Master. The point is that *kōan* exercise in Zen polishes my inner eye to enable me to become one with every situation encountered in daily life, and to be able to respond to that situation not based on some thought or ideology or some calculated set of norms, but right from the source of my very being, in a way that is demanded by the situation. "I was hungry, and you gave me to eat, I was thirsty, you gave me to drink, I was a stranger, and you welcomed me" (Mt. 25:35).

Such a way of responding to every situation in daily life is pictured for us in the image of Kuan-Yin with a Thousand Hands. Kuan-Yin, called Kannon or Kanzeon in Japanese (literally meaning "Perceiver, or Hearer of the Cries of the World") is the bodhisattva par excellence in Buddhism, who in her enlightened state perceives the emptiness of all existence. (Cf. *Heart Sūtra* on Liberating Wisdom.) Incidentally, in the original Sanskrit, *Avalokiteśvara* is of male gender, but this bodhisattva evolved later as a female form, embodying the aspect of compassion that naturally flows out of the wisdom of enlightenment.

Besides the thousand hands, the bodhisattva is portrayed also as possessed of eleven faces, signifying her ability to perceive everything in all directions. Also, if one looks closely, each of the thousand hands is meant to perform a distinct function, such as allaying fear (diagram a), wiping out evil (diagram b), fighting enemies of injustice (diagram c), driving out demons (diagram d), healing fevers and all kinds of diseases (diagrams e and f), setting the dharma wheel in motion, calling forth the inner religious drive in living beings that lead them to see the fleetingness of existence and to seek the wisdom of enlightenment (diagram g), and many more.

In short, in whatever situation of suffering, illness, difficulty or need living beings find themselves, the bodhisattva "extends a hand" in a way that answers the call of the situation. "I was hungry and you gave me to eat, thirsty and you gave me to drink, a stranger and you welcomed me."

Kuan-Yin with a Thousand Arms is no other than the mode of being of one who has reached the ultimate goal in Zen, which is a total emptying of oneself leading to that total liberation whereby one's whole being is given over for others as they are encountered. "This is my body which is given up for you."

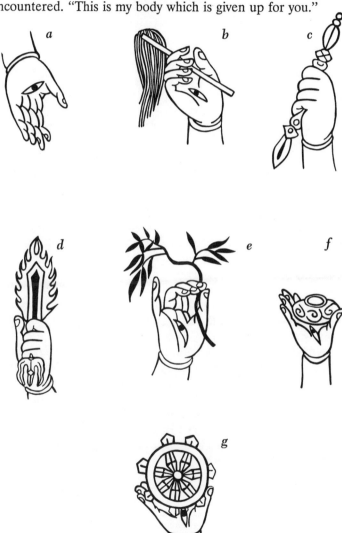

Epilogue

Zen Spirituality

Attuning to the Breath of God

Posture, breathing, and silencing the mind are the three key elements of *zazen* or Zen sitting practice. First, one assumes a bodily position conducive to prolonged stillness, preferably taking a lotus position, but most important, keeping one's back straight. Second, one regulates the breathing, paying attention with each in-breath and out-breath. Third, one silences the mind by not dwelling on any particular thought or sensation, but by being fully present in the *here* and *now*, as one sits, paying attention to every breath.*

Now in the Christian tradition, the term *spirituality* derives from the Greek *pneuma* or spirit, which in turn derives from the Hebrew *rûah*, "the breath of God." Throughout the Old Testament the Breath of God plays a key function in all the significant events of salvation history, beginning with the act of creation itself (Gen. 1:2). The Breath of God is the very dynamic presence of God himself, a presence that gives life to all and renews the face of the earth.

*For details about Zen practice, see Philip Kapleau, *The Three Pillars of Zen* (Boston: 1965). Kapleau's accounts are based on the teaching of Yasutani Hakuun Rōshi, Yamada Kōun Rōshi's teacher in the dharma, and give a good description of the Zen practice at San-un Zen Hall in Kamakura, Japan. Also, see Sr. Elaine MacInnes, O.L.M., *Teaching Zen to Christians* (Manila: Zen Center for Oriental Spirituality, 1986).

The whole life of Jesus is permeated with this dynamic presence, the breath of God, from the time of his conception in the womb of the Blessed Mother — "The Holy Spirit will come upon you, and the power of the Most High will overshadow you" (Lk. 1:35), — up to the completion of his life on the cross when he gave up the spirit back to the Father (Jn. 19:30).

The theme of Jesus' whole life is summarized in the quotation from Isaiah that he read at the synagogue in his hometown:

> *The Spirit of the Lord is upon me,*
> *because he has anointed me to preach good news to the*
>   *poor.*
> *He sent me to proclaim release to the captives,*
> *and the recovery of sight to the blind.*
> *To set at liberty those who are oppressed,*
> *to proclaim the acceptable year of the Lord.*
>   *(Lk. 4:18-19)*

In other words, the key to understanding the life of Jesus is in his being replete with the Breath of God through and through; his whole existence is vivified, guided, inspired and fulfilled in it.

For Christians, spirituality is nothing other than a life in attunement to the Spirit, the Breath of God, wherein one lets one's total being be taken up in its dynamic presence, be guided by it in reading the signs of the times and in responding to every situation.

Paying attention to one's breathing in Zen, then, is seen not simply as a physical exercise that keeps one concentrated on one point, but the very abandonment of one's total being to this Breath of God, here and now. It is letting one's whole self be possessed by the Spirit of God, to be vivified, guided, inspired and fulfilled in it.

And as one is "overshadowed" by the Spirit, one's whole being becomes offered for God's dynamic liberating action in history. To preach good news to the poor. To proclaim release to the captives. To set at liberty those who are oppressed.

One asks then, concretely, who are the poor, the captives, the oppressed? The answer can only come from a reading of the concrete situation of the world today, in other words, an actual exposure to the situations of poverty, oppression, exploitation and ecological destruction, that many living beings are trapped in today. To place oneself on the side of the *victims* of the structural and actual violence that is going on in today's world will provide us the key to answer this question. And only if we are able to recognize, in the concrete, the poor, the captives, the oppressed, will we be able to ask the next set of questions: What is the nature of the *good news* that is to be preached to the poor? the *release* to be proclaimed to the captives? the *liberty* to be realized for the oppressed?

In order to tackle this second set of questions, one cannot remain on a naive level of simply responding to each situation as it arises on the surface level, as bandaging every wound or treating every pain with a mere external remedy. No, a total healing calls for an examination of the causes of the sickness, and the taking of steps to enable the whole organism to move on the way to recovery. In short, we need sophisticated methods of social analysis of our present contemporary world situation in the different contexts in which we find ourselves, and a well-considered program of responding to the needs as revealed by that social analysis.*

But the point here is, whatever follows in the light of such social analysis as the required modes of action to be taken in responding to the given situations, it is all done simply as a response to the call of the Spirit upon whom one has abandoned one's whole existence.

Thus the concrete action taken as one abandons one's being to God's liberating work in history is simply the natural flow based on attuning oneself to the Spirit of God, letting oneself be totally possessed by it, here and now, with every in-breath, out-breath.

The Christian enlightened person, made aware of his or her total nothingness before the face of God, can sum up his or her whole existence thus: "The Spirit of the Lord is upon me."

*On this, see Joe Holland and Peter Henriot, S.J., *Social Analysis: Linking Faith and Justice* (Maryknoll, NY: Orbis, 1983).

Index